Introduction

So much has happened in the world since this play was first performed in 1985. And yet so little has happened, too. I guess there can't be too many people around who still don't know what AIDS is, and how serious, and how awful. And if that's so, why has there been so little progress, and such reluctance, toward curing it, and eradicating it, and confronting it?

These, of course, are the very same questions *The Normal Heart* asks. One would think the great number of people now infected, and facing infection, would have helped speed the research, the necessary government attention. But it hasn't. In fact, relatively little has changed at all in this department. Oh, more money is being allocated round and about for AIDS, but not nearly enough, and certainly not commensurate with the extent of the problem. According to Dr. William Haseltine of Harvard University, *one billion* people will be HIV positive by the year 2020. It will take a lot more than is presently being done to stop this inexorable march of death..

AIDS is now truly a plague. When I first became involved in fighting it, there were only 41 cases that had been announced.

I have learned a great deal during these plague years. I have learned that while people can be wonderful, their governments can be more hideous and hateful than can be imagined – certainly than I could ever have imagined. I have learned that huge numbers of human beings can actually be left to die. There is no doubt in my mind that AIDS is intentional genocide. It is – and has been since the beginning – red tape and government inaction (most specifically the governments of the United States, under the presidencies of Ronald Reagan, George Bush, and Bill Clinton) that have been and are preventing the eradication of AIDS; it is not the dearth of scientific knowledge. That is a terrible condemnation of one's country, but I make it emphatically.

It is amazing to me, even today, when I reread this play, or see a performance, how much the same situation still exists as the period I dramatized. I could have written much of this play last year, or yesterday. It is awful to face this realization, and awful to be reminded of the many friends now dead whose lives gave me the inspiration to write this. The characters of Craig, David, Bruce, Felix, Grady – now all dead. Emma herself (Dr. Linda Laubenstein of New York University Medical Center) has also died, from a stroke, fighting for her patients and their lives and rights until the end. From the original New York cast, Brad Davis has died, and

Larry Lott and Billy DeAcutis. Death, death, death – everywhere around us, omnipresent. We have learned to live with it, somehow. We don't ask why or how. We just go on. As best we can.

Everything in this play happened. When I started out writing it, I took more liberties. But I felt, as I wrote on, that taking liberties was not an option. I felt I couldn't 'make up' things, when the truth was so dreadful and sad. These were real people who were trying so hard to accomplish something, even in their violent disagreements and their hasty love. There was a real Felix and there was a real Bruce and a real Emma. And I, the real Ned – who for some reason completely incomprehensible to me is still alive – miss them all awfully.

Gay Men's Health Crisis, Inc. – the organization Bruce and Ned and Mickey and Tommy are fighting to establish – is now a huge bureaucracy, with hundreds of employees and an annual budget of some $25 million. It is, in fact, the largest AIDS service organization anywhere in the world. When I pass its huge modern office building in Manhattan, it's hard for me not to remember the first meeting we had in my living room and the tiny office that held our first efforts. I get angry with GMHC quite often (in fact my fights with their various boards of directors are well known) because the organization is still so conservative and timid. Sometimes I even say I'm not proud of it at all. But secretly, I take pride in its existence. It's certainly better for this plague that it's there than if it wasn't. Too, while passing by, or walking its corridors, it's hard not to think of Paul Popham – the real Bruce Niles – and remember how hard he fought to bring this edifice into reality. He may not have wanted to be 'political' in those beginning years, but he certainly became the true fighter long before he died. And on his death bed, we made our peace.

Many people have asked me to identify the real Felix Turner. Since he had not been a part of 'our crowd', and was not involved in any of these community political battles, he was not known by many of my other friends who were. And since he'd been married, with a wife and children before he came to New York, he had few gay friends in the city before we fell in love and moved in together. I have almost named him a few times, over the years, each time finding myself – quite uncharacteristically – shutting up. Felix is the only thing I *haven't* blabbed on about endlessly. I'm not certain I know why. (Dr. Laubenstein would never come and see a production of the play. 'I just don't want to', was all she'd say to me about it. I had just got her to agree to at least meet Barbra Streisand, who is going to play her in the film version, when she died.) I think I just want to keep him for my very own. And I think he'd want it this way, too. So, here is someone I am not going to 'out'.

LARRY KRAMER

Larry Kramer is a writer and AIDS treatment activist. In 1981, with five friends, he founded Gay Men's Health Crisis, now the world's largest AIDS service establishment; and in 1987 he founded ACT UP, the AIDS advocacy and protest organisation.

Graduating from Yale University in 1957, he worked in films and then moved to London where he produced his own screenplay adaptation of D.H. Lawrence's *Women in Love*, nominated for an Academy Award, with Glenda Jackson receiving an Oscar for Best Actress.

His play about the early years of AIDS, *The Normal Heart* (1985), has had over six hundred productions all over the world and holds the record for the longest-running play at Joseph Papp's Public Theater in New York. The British premiere at the Royal Court Theatre, starring Martin Sheen, broke all box-office records there before transferring to the West End. It has been acquired for filming by Barbra Streisand and Columbia Pictures.

Subsequent work includes *Just Say No, a Play about a Farce* (1988), a book of non-fiction, *Reports from the holocaust: the making of an AIDS activist* (1989, Penguin), and *Faggots* (1978, Minerva), still one of the best-selling of all gay novels.

The Destiny of Me (1992), a companion play to *The Normal Heart*, has also been acquired for filming by Barbra Streisand and Columbia. Runner-up for the Pulitzer Prize in Drama, it also won an Obie, the Lucille Lortel Award for Best Play, and the Hull-Warriner Award of the Dramatists Guild. The British premiere at the Leicester Haymarket was directed by Simon Callow, who also played the lead.

Kramer is currently at work on *The American People*, a long novel about the plague. He is HIV positive, was born in Connecticut, grew up in Washington, D.C., and lives in New York.

Other Volumes in this Series

LARRY KRAMER

THE NORMAL HEART

NICK HERN BOOKS
London

A Nick Hern Book

The Normal Heart first published in this edition in Great Britain
in 1993 as a paperback original by Nick Hern Books Limited,
14 Larden Road, London W3 7ST. Originally published in
the United States and Canada in 1985. Originally published
in Great Britain in 1986, revised in 1987.
Reprinted 1998

A CIP catalogue record for this book is available from the
British Library

ISBN 1 85459 285 8

Typeset by Country Setting, Woodchurch, Kent TN26 3TB
Printed by Cox & Wyman Ltd, Reading, Berkshire

ACKNOWLEDGEMENTS
Cover image of Martin Sheen in the British premiere production
based on a photograph by John Haynes.
Portion of 'September 1, 1939', copyright © 1940 by W.H. Auden,
reprinted by permission of Faber and Faber Ltd, from *The English
Auden: Poems, Essays and Dramatic Writings 1927-1939*, edited
by Edward Mendelson

I am very pleased that Nick Hern is bringing back this play for British readers. He was its first publisher, when he was at Methuen, and he has always been its ardent fan. Together with its companion play, *The Destiny of Me*, I have tried to record my life as it was lived and formed during these years of AIDS. They have been in every way the most remarkable of years, hideous, heartbreaking, inspirational, and filled with love and hate. There was nothing else I could write about and nothing else I want to write about until I, too, am dead.

I conceive of *The Normal Heart* and *The Destiny of Me* as the first two plays in a trilogy. I hope I shall have the strength and time to write the final play, which will somehow put closure to this story, this story of my life and times.

Larry Kramer
August 1993

Original New York Production of
THE NORMAL HEART
by New York Shakespeare Festival

Produced by Joseph Papp

Larry Kramer's *The Normal Heart* is a play in the great tradition of
Western drama. In taking a burning social issue and holding it up
to public and private scrutiny so that it reverberates with the social
and personal implications of that issue, *The Normal Heart* reveals
its origins in the theatre of Sophocles, Euripides, and Shakespeare.
In his moralistic fervour, Larry Kramer is a first cousin to
nineteenth-century Ibsen and twentieth-century Odets and other
radical writers of the 1930s. Yet, at the heart of *The Normal Heart,*
the element that gives this powerful political play its essence, is
love – love holding firm under fire, put to the ultimate test, facing
and overcoming our greatest fear: death.

I love the ardour of this play, its howling, its terror and its
kindness. It makes me very proud to be its producer and caretaker.

Joseph Papp

About the New York Production

The New York Shakespeare Festival production at the Public Theater was conceived as exceptionally simple. Little furniture was used: a few wooden office chairs, a desk, a table, a sofa, and an old battered hospital gurney that found service as an examining table, a bench in City Hall, and a place for coats in the organisation's old office. As the furniture found itself doing double duty in different scenes, so did the doorways built into the set's back wall. In many instances, the actors used the theatre itself for entrances and exits.

The walls of the set, made of construction-site plywood, were whitewashed. Everywhere possible, on this set and upon the theatre walls too, facts and figures and names were painted, in black, simple lettering.

Here are some of the things we painted on our walls:

1. Principal place was given to the latest total number of AIDS cases nationally – AND COUNTING. (For example, on 1 August 1985, the figure read 12,062.)

   As the Centers for Disease Control revise all figures regularly, so did we, crossing out old numbers and placing the new figure just beneath it.

2. This was also done for states and major cities.

3. EPIDEMIC OFFICIALLY DECLARED JUNE 5, 1981.

4. MAYOR KOCH: $75,000 – MAYOR FEINSTEIN: $16,000,000. (For public education and community services.)

5. 'TWO MILLION AMERICANS ARE INFECTED – ALMOST 10 TIMES THE OFFICIAL ESTIMATES' – Dr Robert Gallo, London *Observer*, 7 April 1985.

6. The number of cases in children.

7. The number of cases in gays and the number of cases in straights, calculated by subtracting the gay and bisexual number from the total CDC figure.

8. The total number of articles on the epidemic written by the following newspapers during the first ten months of 1984:

The San Francisco Chronicle	163
The New York Times	41
The Los Angeles Times	37
The Washington Post	24

9. During the first nineteen months of the epidemic, *The New York Times* wrote about it a total of seven times:
    1. July 3, 1981, page 20 (41 cases reported by CDC)
    2. August 29, 1981, page 9 (107 cases)
    3. May 11, 1982, Section III, page 1 (335 cases)
    4. June 18, 1982, Section II, page 8 (approximately 430 cases)
    5. August 8, 1982, page 31 (505 cases)
    6. January 6, 1983, Section II, page 17 (approximately 891 cases)
    7. February 6, 1983, Magazine (The 'Craig Claiborne' article.) (958 cases)

10. During the three months of the Tylenol scare in 1982, *The New York Times* wrote about it a total of 54 times: October 1, 2, 3, 4, 5, 6, 7, 8, 9, 10, 11, 12, 13, 14, 15, 16, 17, 18, 19, 20, 21, 22, 23, 24, 25, 26, 27, 28, 29, 30, 31, November 2, 5, 6, 9, 12, 17, 21, 22, 25, December 1, 2, 3, 4, 8, 10, 14, 15, 19, 25, 27, 28, 29, 30. Four of these articles appeared on the front page. Total number of cases: 7.

11. Government research at the National Institutes of Health did not commence in reality until January 1983, eighteen months after the same government had declared the epidemic.

12. One entire wall contained this passage:
    'There were two alternative strategies a Jewish organization could adopt to get the American government to initiate action on behalf of the imperilled Jews of Europe. It could co-operate with the government officials, quietly trying to convince them that rescue of Jews should be one of the objectives of the war, or it could try to pressure the government into initiating rescue by using embarrassing public attention and rallying public opinion to that end.

    The American Jewish Committee chose the former strategy and clung to it tenaciously.

    From the very onset of Jewish crises, the Committee responded to each new Nazi outrage by practising their traditional style of discreet 'backstairs' diplomacy.

    With each worsening event, the Committee reacted by contacting yet another official or re-visiting the same ones to call their attention to the new situation.

    The Jewish delegates were usually politely informed that the matter was being given the 'most earnest attention.'

They were still trying to persuade the same officials when the war ended.'

From *American Jewry During the Holocaust*, prepared for the American Jewish Commission on the Holocaust, 1984, edited by Seymour Maxwell Finger (reprinted by permission).

13. Announcement of the discovery of 'the virus' in France: January 1983. Announcement of the 'discovery' of 'the virus' in Washington: April 1984.

14. The public education budget for 1985 at the U.S. Department of Health and Human Services: $120,000.

15. Vast expanses of wall were covered with lists of names, much like the names one might find on a war memorial, such as the Vietnam Memorial in Washington.

The Normal Heart was first presented on 21 April 1985 at the Public Theater in New York City, New York; a New York Shakespeare Festival Production, it was produced by Joseph Papp. It had the following cast:

in order of appearance

CRAIG DONNER	Michael Santoro
MICKEY MARCUS	Robert Dorfman
NED WEEKS	Brad Davis
DAVID	Lawrence Lott
DR EMMA BROOKNER	Concetta Tomei
BRUCE NILES	David Allen Brooks
FELIX TURNER	D.W. Moffett
BEN WEEKS	Phillip Richard Allen
TOMMY BOATWRIGHT	William DeAcutis
HIRAM KEEBLER	Lawrence Lott
GRADY	Michael Santoro
EXAMINING DOCTOR	Lawrence Lott
ORDERLY	Lawrence Lott
ORDERLY	Michael Santoro

Director	Michael Lindsay-Hogg
Scenery	Eugene Lee, Keith Raywood
Lighting	Natasha Katz
Costumes	Bill Walker
Associate Producer	Jason Steven Cohen

The Normal Heart had its British premiere at the Royal Court Theatre, London on 20 March 1986, with the following cast:

in order of appearance

CRAIG DONNER	Kerry Shale
MICKEY MARCUS	Joris Stuyck
DAVID	Stuart Fox
NED WEEKS	Martin Sheen
DR EMMA BROOKNER	Frances Tomelty
BRUCE NILES	John Terry
FELIX TURNER	Paul Jesson
BEN WEEKS	Richard Kane
TOMMY BOATWRIGHT	Stuart Milligan
HIRAM KEEBLER	Stuart Fox
LENNIE	Stuart Fox
GRADY	Kerry Shale
EXAMINING DOCTOR	Stuart Fox
ORDERLY	Kerry Shale
ORDERLY	Stuart Fox

Director	David Hayman
Designer	Geoff Rose
Lighting Designer	Gerry Jenkinson

This production transferred to the Albery Theatre on 20 May 1986 with Tom Hulce, and then John Shea, replacing Martin Sheen.

The action of this play takes place between July 1981 and May 1984 in New York City.

Scenes and approximate dates

Act One

Act Two

The windiest militant trash
Important Persons shout
Is not so crude as our wish:
What mad Nijinsky wrote
About Diaghilev
Is true of the normal heart;
For the error bred in the bone
Of each woman and each man
Craves what it cannot have,
Not universal love
But to be loved alone.

All I have is a voice
To undo the folded lie,
The romantic lie in the brain
Of the sensual man-in-the-street
And the lie of Authority
Whose buildings grope the sky:
There is no such thing as the State
And no one exists alone;
Hunger allows no choice
To the citizen or the police;
We must love one another or die.

From 'September 1, 1939'
W.H. AUDEN

ACT ONE

Scene One

The office of DR EMMA BROOKNER. *Several* MEN *are sitting in the waiting area. As the lights come up, one of them,* DAVID, *who is wearing a Hawaiian sports shirt, goes into the inner office.* MICKEY MARCUS, *in his late 30s, intense and a bit unkempt and* CRAIG DONNER, *in his mid-20s and very appealing, remain.* CRAIG *walks nervously about the office. He is not feeling well.*

CRAIG. I don't think much of her interior decorator.

MICKEY. Come sit down.

CRAIG. Patients' rights. We demand prettier offices. Maybe she's a terrible doctor. Maybe she doesn't care. Maybe she has bad taste. Maybe she isn't Jewish. Did you see his spots?

MICKEY. You don't have those. Do you?

CRAIG *shakes his head 'No'.*

Then you don't have anything to worry about.

CRAIG. She said they can be inside you, too.

MICKEY. They're not inside you.

CRAIG. They're inside me. Where's Bruce? He said he'd be here.

MICKEY. Bruce is coming? How many people do you need to come to get some test results?

CRAIG. I know something's wrong.

MICKEY. Craig, please don't be so negative.

CRAIG. I'm tired all the time. I wake up in swimming pools of sweat. She felt me all over and said I was swollen. I'm all swollen, like something ready to explode. Thank you for coming with me. You're a good friend, Mickey. I always get freaked out when I don't feel well.

DAVID, *the man in the Hawaiian shirt, comes out of the inner office. Now we can see that there are big purple spots on his face and arms. He looks like he has just received word of a sentence of death, which in effect he has. He stands there numb.*

DAVID. They keep getting bigger and bigger. And they don't go away.

MICKEY *and* CRAIG *just stare at him. He starts to walk out, then remembers:*

Whoever is next is supposed to go in.

MICKEY *(hugging* CRAIG*).* Good luck.

CRAIG *goes in.* DAVID *starts walking out, but stops as* NED WEEKS *comes in.* NED *is in his mid-40s.* DAVID *recognises him, but* NED *is not certain where he knows* DAVID *from.*

DAVID. I sold you a ceramic pig once at Maison France on Bleecker Street.

NED. Yes, I remember. Somebody I was friends with then collects pigs and you had the biggest pig I'd ever seen outside of a real pig.

DAVID. I'm her twenty-eighth case and sixteen of them are dead.

NED. I'm sorry.

DAVID. I can't even go home to get my things. I've got to check in right now.

NED. Please tell me your name again.

DAVID. David. I sold you a ceramic pig. I don't have many friends. None of them will understand. There's no one I can tell.

NED . . . . Is there anything you'd like me to do?

DAVID. I don't think there's anything that can be done for me.

NED. I'll bet there are.

DAVID. Power of positive thinking and all that? *(He leaves.)*

NED *(who has seen and nodded to* MICKEY, *comes to him). I* think I just put my foot in it.

MICKEY. You should be used to that.

NED. What do you say? Mickey, what the fuck is going on?

MICKEY. I don't know to both questions.

NED. Are you all right?

MICKEY. I'm fine. What about you?

NED. I feel okay. We never seem able to quite get our act together. Now this.

MICKEY. We've been getting our act together just fine. Why is it our fault already?

NED. I didn't say it was our fault.

MICKEY (*not unkindly*). For a change.

NED. What's the political word going to be about this?

MICKEY. I don't know.

NED. It looks to me to be a very hot potato for you guys in the movement.

MICKEY. If it isn't, maybe you'll find a way to make it one. Is that why you're here?

NED. Just want to ask some questions, Mick, to find out more. The *Times* didn't say very much but what it said is scary. Isn't that why you're here, too?

MICKEY (*nodding to the inner office*). Craig is convinced he's got it.

NED. Craig Donner?

MICKEY. But he's always been a terrible hypochondriac.

NED. He's in there?

MICKEY *nods*. NED *shivers*.

MICKEY. I guess you know that Craig is with Bruce now. You know Bruce Niles? The gorgeous clone that everyone's always after? Well, Craig's got him. Craig was awfully miserable after you threw him out - and now look: he's got Robert Redford.

NED. It shows you there is a God. I didn't throw him out. It just wasn't working.

MICKEY. How could anybody not love Craig?

NED. There's no blame. I didn't love him. How's John?

MICKEY. John? John who?

NED. You've had so many I never remember their last names.

MICKEY. Oh, you mean John. I'm with Gregory now. I've been with Gregory for ten months. Gregory O'Connor.

NED. You mean the old gay activist?

MICKEY. He's younger than you are!

NED. Mickey, that's very nice.

MICKEY. He's not even Jewish, but don't tell my Rabbi. Isn't it funny we should become lovers after all these years together in the movement?

NED. It is. You guys have never exactly stood for happily married life.

MICKEY. We're only lovers and live together. We're certainly not faithful to each other too. You're still the romantic under all that bluster. I'll bet you're still single. *(When NED doesn't respond.) You* do make it difficult, you know, walking around with 'Do Not Touch' signs all over you. Don't you know you're a catch? Successful, rich, reasonably attractive.

NED. I am not . . . rich.

MICKEY. Are you snooping around all this just to write about it?

NED. I don't know. I haven't thought about it. What's wrong with that?

MICKEY. Nothing I guess. I'm certainly going to write about it in my health column in the *Native*. I'm afraid to put it in the stuff I write at work. I'm still at the Health Department, thank goodness, there have been so'many cutbacks.

NED. Why are you afraid?

MICKEY. This city doesn't exactly show a burning interest in gay health.

CRAIG comes out of the inner office. He has obviously just been told the worst.

CRAIG *(sees NED and turns to MICKEY)*. Did Bruce get here yet?

NED. Hello, Craig.

CRAIG. You always show up for the good times.

NED. I'm sorry. If that's any use. It isn't, I know.

CRAIG. I'm going to die. That's the bottom line of what she's telling me.

NED tries to embrace him, but CRAIG pulls away: then he rushes into his arms.

Ned, I'm so scared. *(He pulls away.)* I have to go home and get my things.

Everyone looks at everyone else, not knowing what else to do or say. MICKEY puts his arm around CRAIG, and they leave. NED stands there alone, shaken by this series of events. Through the open door, in a motorised wheelchair, comes DR EMMA BROOKNER. She is in her mid-to-late 30s, and wears a white doctor's coat.

EMMA. Who are you?

NED. Ned Weeks. I spoke to you on the phone after the *Times* article.

EMMA. You're the writer fellow who's scared. I'm scared too. *(She goes to the desk and finds NED's folder.)* I hear you've got a big mouth.

NED. Is big mouth a symptom?

EMMA. No, a cure. Come on in and take your clothes off.

NED. I'm only here to ask some questions and get some information.

EMMA. You're gay, aren't you?

NED. Yes.

EMMA. Then take your clothes off. *(She has started putt-putting back into her office.)*

NED. What do you think is happening?

EMMA. I don't know.

She heads into her office. An examining table under a bright light appears. NED starts taking off his clothes and hanging them on a clotheshorse.

Are you all right? You look a little shaky.

NED. In just a couple of minutes I've seen two people I know be told . . . something.

EMMA. I know the feeling.

NED. The article said there isn't any cure.

EMMA. Not even any good clues yet. *(As he hesitates with his undershorts.)* Don't be nervous. I've seen more men than you have.

NED decides to leave his shorts on. EMMA will proceed to examine his skin minutely, first while he stands, and then while he is lying down on the table. She adjusts a magnifying light on a band around her head and also the overhead light as needed.

She has moved her wheelchair to just in front of him, which makes him jump back a bit nervously.

Stand still. And even if they found out tomorrow what's happening, it takes years to find out how to cure and prevent anything.

NED. What . . . do you personally think is happening?

EMMA. You're not very good at new questions, are you? Okay, I don't know what's happening but I do know this disease is the most insidious killer I've ever seen or studied or heard about. And I think it's on the rampage. And I think we're seeing only the tip of the iceberg. And I'm frightened that nobody important . . . Lift up your arm . . . is going to give a damn because it seems to be happening mostly to gay men. Who cares if a faggot dies? Does it occur to you to do anything about it? Personally?

NED. Me?

EMMA. Somebody's got to do something.

NED. Wouldn't it be better coming from you?

EMMA. Doctors are funny animals. They're extremely conservative; they try to stay out of anything that smells politically, and this smells. Bad. As soon as you start screaming you get treated like a nut case. Maybe you know that. And then you're ostracised, just when you need cooperation most.

NED. Nobody listens for very long anyway. There's a new disease of the month every day.

EMMA. This hospital sent its report of our first cases to the medical journals over a year ago. *The New England Journal of Medicine* has finally published it, and last week, which brought you running, the *Times* ran something on some inside page. Very inside page twenty. If you remember, Legionnaires' Disease, toxic-shock, they both hit the front page of the *Times* the minute they happened. And stayed there until somebody did something. The front page of the *Times* has a way of inspiring action. Lie down.

NED. They won't even use the word 'gay' unless it's in a direct quote. To them we're still homosexuals. That's like still calling blacks Negroes. The *Times* has always had trouble writing about anything gay.

EMMA. Then how is anyone going to know what's happening? And what precautions to take? Someone's going to have to tell the gay population fast.

NED. You've been living with this for over a year? Where's the Mayor? Where's the Health Department?

EMMA. They know about it. You have a Commissioner of Health who got burned with the Swine Flu epidemic, declaring an emergency when there wasn't one. The government appropriated $150 million for that mistake. You have a Mayor who's a bachelor and I assume afraid of being perceived as too friendly to anyone gay. And who is also out to protect a billion-dollar-a-year tourist industry. He's not about to tell the world there's an epidemic menacing his city. And don't ask me about the President. Is the Mayor gay?

NED. If he is, like J. Edgar Hoover, who would want him?

EMMA. Have you had any of the symptoms?

NED. I've had most of the sexually transmitted diseases the article
said come first. A lot of us have. You don't know what it's
been like since the sexual revolution hit this country. It's been
crazy, gay or straight.

EMMA. What makes you think I don't know? Any fever, weight
loss, night sweats, diarrhoea, swollen glands, white patches in
your mouth, loss of energy, shortness of breath, chronic cough?

NED. No. But those could happen with a lot of things, couldn't
they?

EMMA. And purple lesions. Sometimes. Which is what I'm
looking for. It's a cancer. There seems to be a strange reaction
in the immune system. It's collapsed. Won't work. Won't fight.
Which is what it's supposed to do. So most of the diseases my
guys are coming down with – and there are some very strange
ones – are caused by germs that wouldn't hurt a baby, not a
baby in New York City anyway. Unfortunately, the immune
system is the system we know least about. So where is this big
mouth I hear you've got.

NED. I have more of a bad temper than a big mouth.

EMMA. Nothing wrong with that. Plenty to get angry about.
Health is a political issue. Everyone's entitled to good medical
care. If you're not getting it, you've got to fight for it. Do you
know this is the only country in the industrialised world besides
South Africa that doesn't guarantee health care for everyone?
Open your mouth. Turn over. One of my staff told me you were
well-known in the gay world and not afraid to say what you
think. That's why I agreed to see you. I don't usually see
patients just off the street without a referral. I haven't got time.
I can't find any gay leaders. I tried calling several gay
organisations. No one ever calls me back. Is anyone out there?

NED. There aren't any organisations strong enough to be useful,
no. Dr Brookner, nobody with a brain gets involved in gay
politics. It's filled with the great unwashed radicals of any
counterculture. That's why there aren't any leaders the majority
will follow. Anyway, you're talking to the wrong person. What
I think is politically incorrect.

EMMA. Why?

NED. Gay is good to that crowd, no matter what. There's no room
for criticism, looking at ourselves critically.

EMMA. What's your main criticism?

NED. I hate how we play victim, when many of us, most of us, don't have to.

EMMA. Then you're exactly what's needed now.

NED. Nobody ever listens. We're not exactly a bunch that knows how to play follow the leader.

EMMA. Maybe they're just waiting for somebody to lead them.

NED. We are. What group isn't?

EMMA. You can get dressed. I can't find what I'm looking for.

NED (*jumping down and starting to dress*). Needed? Needed for what? What is it exactly you're trying to get me to do?

EMMA. Tell gay men to stop having sex.

NED. What?

EMMA. Someone has to. Why not you?

NED. It is a preposterous request.

EMMA. It only sounds harsh. Wait a few more years, it won't sound so harsh.

NED. Do you realise that you are talking about millions of men who have singled out promiscuity to be their principal political agenda, the one they'd die before abandoning. How do you deal with that?

EMMA. Tell them they may die.

NED. You tell them!

EMMA. Are you saying you guys can't relate to each other in a non-sexual way?

NED. It's more complicated than that. For a lot of guys it's not easy to meet each other in any other way. It's a way of connecting – which becomes an addiction. And then they're caught in the web of peer pressure to perform and perform. Are you sure this is spread by having sex?

EMMA. Long before we isolated the hepatitis viruses we knew about the diseases they caused and had a good idea of how they got around. I think I'm right about this. I am seeing more cases each week than the week before. I figure that by the end of the year the number will be doubling every six months. That's something over a thousand cases by next June. Half of them will be dead. Your two friends I've just diagnosed? One of them will be dead. Maybe both of them.

NED. And you want me to tell every gay man in New York to stop having sex?

EMMA. Who said anything about just New York?

NED. You want me to tell every gay man across the country –

EMMA. Across the world ! That's the only way this disease will stop spreading.

NED. Dr Brookner, isn't that just a tiny bit unrealistic?

EMMA. Mr Weeks, if having sex can kill you, doesn't anybody with half a brain stop fucking? But perhaps you've never lost anything. Goodbye.

BRUCE NILES, *an exceptionally handsome man in his late thirties, rushes in carrying* CRAIG, *helped by* MICKEY.

BRUCE *(calling off)*. Where do I go? Where do I go?

EMMA. Quickly – put him on the table! What happened?

BRUCE. He was coming out of the building and he started running to me and then he . . . collapsed to the ground.

EMMA. What is going on inside your bodies!

CRAIG *starts to convulse.* BRUCE, MICKEY *and* NED *restrain him.*

Gently. Hold on to his chin.

She takes a tongue depressor and holds CRAIG '*s tongue flat: she checks the pulse in his neck she looks into his eyes for vital signs that he is coming around:* CRAIG's *convulsions stop.*

You the lover?

BRUCE. Yes.

EMMA. What's your name?

BRUCE. Bruce Niles, ma'am.

EMMA. How's your health?

BRUCE. Fine. Why – is it contagious?

EMMA. I think so.

MICKEY. Then why haven't you come down with it?

EMMA *(moving towards a telephone)*. Because it seems to have a very long incubation period and require close intimacy. Niles? You were Reinhard Holz's lover?

BRUCE. How did you know that? I haven't seen him in a couple of years.

EMMA *(dialling the hospital emergency number)*. He died three weeks ago. Brookner. Emergency. Set up a room immediately.

She hangs up.

BRUCE. We were only boyfriends for a couple months.

MICKEY. It's like some sort of plague.

EMMA. There's always a plague. Of one kind or another. I've had it since I was a kid. Mr Weeks, I don't think your friend is going to live for very long.

Scene Two

FELIX TURNER's *desk at the* New York Times. FELIX is *in his early 30s and is conservatively dressed, stylish and neat, in a suit and tie. He is completely masculine, outgoing, energetic.*

NED . . . . Mr Turner?

FELIX *(waving him away without looking up).* Bad timing! *(Something makes him look up.)* Mister?

NED *(offering him his hand).* My name is Ned Weeks.

FELIX. Yes, I remember.

NED. Remember what?

FELIX. I saw your picture on a book jacket. You caught me at a rough moment. I'm very late for my deadline.

NED. I've been told you're gay,

FELIX *does a quick doubletake and turns to see if anyone is within earshot.*

and you might be able to help get important information in the *Times* about . . .

FELIX. You've been told? Who told you?

NED. The grapevine.

FELIX. Here I thought everyone saw me as the Clint Eastwood of West Forty-third Street. What kind of vital information?

NED. You read the article about this new disease?

FELIX. Yes, I read it. I wondered how long before I'd hear from somebody. Why does everyone gay always think I run *The New York Times?* I can't help you . . . with this.

NED. I'm sorry to hear that. What would you suggest I do?

FELIX. Take your pick. I've got twenty-three parties, fourteen gallery openings, thirty-seven new restaurants, twelve new discos, one hundred and five spring collections . . . Anything sound interesting?

NED. No one here wants to write another article. I've talked to half a dozen reporters and editors and the guy who wrote the first piece.

FELIX. That's true. They won't want to write about it. And I can't. We're very departmentalised. You wouldn't want science to write about sweaters, would you?

NED. It is a very peculiar feeling having to go out and seek support from the straight world for something gay.

FELIX. I wouldn't know about that. I just write about gay designers and gay discos and gay chefs and gay rock stars and gay photographers and gay models and gay celebrities and gay everything. I just don't call them gay. Isn't that enough for doing my bit?

NED. No – I don't think it's going to be.

FELIX. I really do have a deadline and you wouldn't like me to get fired; who would write about us at all?

NED. Guys like you give me a pain in the ass. *(He starts out.)*

FELIX. Are you in the book?

NED. Yes.

Scene Three

The law office of BEN WEEKS. BEN *is* NED's *older brother, about 50, and he is always dressed in a suit and tie, which* NED *never is.* NED *loves* BEN *more than anyone in the world and his approval is essential to him.* BEN *is busy with some papers as* NED, *sitting on the opposite side of the desk, waits for him.*

BEN. Isn't a little early to get overwrought? Statistically your chances of remaining healthy improve every time someone else comes down with anything. Where would you like to have lunch today, my young brother?

NED. Don't you be like that, too.

BEN *(looking up)*. What have I done now?

NED. We went out to Fire Island – Bruce, a friend of mine and I –

and all night long, at the most popular disco, from thousands of men, we collected the grand sum of $124.

BEN. You can read that as either an indication that it's a beginning and will improve and you must persevere, or as a portent that heads will stay in the sand. My prediction is that heads stay in the sand. Sign these.

BEN *hands* NED *a batch of papers, which* NED *signs automatically and without question.*

NED. Because so many gay people are in the closet?

BEN. Because people don't like to be frightened. When people are scared, they don't behave well. It's called denial.

NED. What are these for?

BEN. I'm getting you more money. As long as you insist upon not working.

NED. I'm not not working.

BEN (*pulls a big roll of architect's drawings from behind his desk and proceeds to unroll them and lay them out on his desk*). You haven't told me where we're going to have lunch.

NED. What in the world are those?

BEN. I've decided to build a house.

NED. What's wrong with the one you're in?

BEN. Nothing. I just want to build me the dream house I've always wanted and so I'm going to.

NED. It looks like a fortress. Does it have a moat? How much is it going to cost?

BEN. I suspect it'll wind up over a million bucks.

NED *whistles.*

But you're not to tell that to anyone. Not even to Sarah. I've found some land in Greenwich, by a little river, completely protected by trees, Ned, it's going to be beautiful.

NED. Doesn't spending a million dollars on a house frighten you? It would scare the shit out of me. Even if I had it.

BEN. You can have a house anytime you want one. You haven't done badly.

NED. Do I detect a tinge of approval – from the big brother who always called me lemon?

BEN. Well, you were a lemon.

NED. I don't want a house.

BEN. Then why have you been searching for one in the country for so many years?

NED. No fun living in one alone.

BEN. There's certainly no law requiring you to do that. Is this . . . Bruce someone you're seeing?

NED. Why thank you for asking. Don't I wish. I see him. He just doesn't see me. Everyone's afraid of me anyway. I frighten them away. It's called the lemon complex.

BEN. I think you're the one who's scared.

NED. You've never said that before.

BEN. Yes, I have. You just didn't hear me. What's the worst thing that could happen to you?

NED. I'd spend a million bucks on a house. Look, Ben . . . I've . . . we've started an organisation. To raise money and spread information and fight any way we can.

BEN. Fight who and what?

NED. I told you. There's this strange new disease . . .

BEN. You're not going to do that full time?

NED. I just want to help it get started and I'll worry about how much time later on.

BEN. It sounds like another excuse to keep from writing.

NED. I knew you'd say that. Look, I was wondering . . . could your law firm incorporate us and get us tax-exempt status and take us on for free, what's it called, *pro bono?* Please.

BEN. *Pro bono* for what? What are you going to do?

NED. I told you – raise money and . . .

BEN. You have to be more specific than that. You have to have a plan.

NED. How about if we say we intend to become a cross between the League of Women Voters and the United States Marines? Is that a good plan?

BEN. Well, we have a committee that decides this sort of thing. I'll have to put it to the committee.

NED. Why can't you just say yes?

BEN. Because we have a committee.

NED. But you're the senior partner and I'm your brother.

BEN. I fail to see what bearing that has on the matter. You're

asking me to ask my partners to give up income that would
ordinarily come into their pocket.

NED. I thought every firm did a certain amount of this sort of
thing. Charity, worthy causes.

BEN. That's true. It's not up to me, however, to select just what
these worthy causes might be.

NED. That's a pity. What did you start the firm for?

BEN. That's one of our rules. It's a democratic firm.

NED. I think I like elitism better. When will you know?

BEN. Know what?

NED. Whether your committee wants to help dying faggots?

BEN. I'll put it before them at the next meeting.

NED. When is that?

BEN. When it is!

NED. When is it? Because if you're not going to do it, I have to
find somebody else.

BEN. You're more than free to do that.

NED. I don't want to do that! I want my brother's fancy famous
big-deal straight law firm to be the first major New York law
firm to do *pro bono* work for a gay cause. That would give me
a great deal of pride. I'm sorry you can't see that. I'm sorry I m
still putting you in a position where you're ashamed of me. I
thought we'd worked all that out years ago.

BEN. I am not ashamed of you! I told you I'm simply not free to
take this on without asking my partners' approval at our next
meeting.

NED. I don't believe that. When is the next meeting?

BEN (*forced to look at his calendar*). Next Monday. Can you wait
until next Monday?

NED. Who else is on the committee?

BEN. What difference does that make?

NED. I'll lobby them. You don't seem like a very sure vote. Is
Nelson on the committee? Norman Ivey? Harvey?

BEN. Norman and Harvey are.

NED. Good.

BEN. Okay? Lemon, where do you want to have lunch today? It's
your turn to pay.

NED. It is not. I paid last week.

BEN. That's simply not true.

NED. Last week was . . . French. You're right. You know you're the only person in the world I can't get mad at and stay mad at. I think my world would come to an end if I didn't have you. And who then would you talk to? *(He embraces BEN.)*

BEN is *embarrassed and recoils a bit.*

BEN. That's true. *(Giving a little bit of an embrace.)*

NED. You're getting better at it.

Scene Four

NED's *apartment. It is stark, modern, all black and white. FELIX comes walking in from another room with a beer, and NED follows, carrying one too.*

FELIX. That's quite a library in there. You read all those books?

NED. Why does everybody ask that?

FELIX. You have a whole room of 'em, you must want to get asked .

NED. I never thought of it that way. Maybe I do. Thank you. But no, of course I haven't. They go out of print and then you can't find them, so I buy them right away.

FELIX. I think you're going to have to face the fact you won't be able to read them all before you die.

NED. I think you're right.

FELIX. You know, I really used to like high tech, but I'm tired of it now. I think I want chintz back again. Don't be insulted.

NED. I'm not. I want chintz back again, too.

FELIX. So here we are – two fellows who want chintz back again. Excuse me for saying so, but you are stiff as starch.

NED. It's been a long time since I've had a date. This is a date, isn't it?

FELIX *nods.*

And on the rare occasion, I was usually the asker.

FELIX. That's what's thrown you off your style: I called and asked.

NED. Some style. Before any second date I usually receive a phone call that starts with 'Now I don't know what you had in mind, but can't we just be friends?'

FELIX. No. Are you glad I'm here?

NED. Oh, I'm pleased as punch you're here. You're very good-looking. What are you doing here?

FELIX. I'll let that tiny bit of self-pity pass for the moment.

NED. It's not self-pity, it's nervousness.

FELIX. It's definitely self-pity. Do you think you're bad-looking?

NED. Where are you from?

FELIX. I'm from Oklahoma. I left home at eighteen and put myself through college. My folks are dead. My dad worked at the refinery in West Tulsa and my mom was a waitress at a luncheonette in Walgreen's.

NED. Isn't it amazing how a kid can come out of all that and wind up on the *Times* dictating taste and style and fashion to the entire world?

FELIX. And we were talking so nicely.

NED. Talking is not my problem. Shutting up is my problem. And keeping my hands off you.

FELIX. You don't have to keep your hands off me. You have very nice hands. Do you have any awkward sexual tendencies you want to tell me about, too? That I'm not already familiar with ?

NED. What are you familiar with?

FELIX. I have found myself pursuing men who hurt me. Before minor therapy. You're not one of those?

NED. No, I'm the runner. I *was* the runner. Until major therapy. After people who didn't want me and away from people who do.

FELIX. Isn't it amazing how a kid can come out of all that analysing everything incessantly down to the most infinitesimal neurosis and still be all alone?

NED. I'm sorry you don't like my Dr Freud. Another ageing Jew who couldn't get laid.

FELIX. Just relax. You'll get laid.

NED. I try being laid-back, assertive, funny, butch . . . What's the point? I don't think there are many gay relationships that work out anyway.

FELIX. It's difficult to imagine you being laid-back. I know a lot of gay relationships that are working out very well.

NED. I guess I never see them.

FELIX. That's because you're a basket case.

NED. Fuck off.

FELIX. What's the matter? Don't you think you're attractive? Don't you like your body?

NED. I don't think anybody really likes their body. I read that somewhere.

FELIX. You know my fantasy has always been to go away and live by the ocean and write twenty-four novels, living with someone just like you with all these books who of course will be right there beside me writing your own twenty-four novels.

NED *(after a beat)*. Me, too.

FELIX. Harold Robbins marries James Michener.

NED. How about Tolstoy and Charles Dickens?

FELIX. As long as Kafka doesn't marry Dostoevsky.

NED. Dostoevsky is my favourite writer.

FELIX. I'll have to try him again.

NED. If you really feel that way, why do you write all that society and party and fancy-ball-gown bullshit?

FELIX. Here we go again. I'll bet you gobble it up every day.

NED. I do. I also know six people who've died. When I came to you a few weeks ago, it was only one.

FELIX. I'm sorry. Is that why you agreed to this date?

NED. Do you know that when Hitler's Final Solution to eliminate the Polish Jews was first mentioned in the *Times* it was on page twenty-eight. And on page six of the *Washington Post*. And the *Times* and *Post* were owned by Jews. What causes silence like that? Why didn't the American Jews help the German Jews get out? Their very own people! Scholars are finally writing honestly about this – I've been doing some research – and it's damning to everyone who was here then: Jewish leadership for being totally ineffective; Jewish organisations for constantly fighting among themselves, unable to co-operate even in the face of death: Zionists versus non-Zionists, Rabbi Wise against Rabbi Silver . . .

FELIX. Is this some sort of special way you talk when you don't want to talk? We were doing so nicely.

NED. We were?

FELIX. Wasn't there an awful lot of anti-Semitism in those days?

Weren't Jews afraid of rubbing people's noses in too much shit?

NED. Yes, everybody has a million excuses for not getting involved. But aren't there moral obligations, moral commandments to try everything possible? Where were the Christian churches, the Pope, Churchill? And don't get me started on Roosevelt . . . How I was brought up to worship him, all Jews were. A clear statement from him would have put everything on the front pages, would have put Hitler on notice. But his administration did its best to stifle publicity at the same time as they clamped down immigration laws forbidding entry, and this famous haven for the oppressed became as inaccessible as Tibet. The title of Treasury Secretary Morgenthau's report to Roosevelt was 'Acquiescence of This Government in the Murder of the Jews,' which he wrote in 1944. Dachau was opened in 1933. Where was everybody for eleven years? And then it was too late.

FELIX. This is turning out to be a very romantic evening.

NED. And don't tell me how much you can accomplish working from the inside! Jewish leaders, relying on their contacts with people in high places, were still, quietly, from the inside, attempting to persuade them when the war was over.

FELIX. What do you want me to say? Do you ever take a vacation?

NED. A vacation. I forgot. That's the great goal, isn't it? A constant Fire Island vacation. Party, party; fuck, fuck. Maybe you can give me a few trendy pointers on what to wear.

FELIX. Boy, you really have a bug up your ass. Look, I'm not going to tell them I'm gay and could I write about the few cases of a mysterious disease that seems to be standing in the way of your kissing me even though there must be half a million gay men in this city who are fine and healthy. Let us please acknowledge the law of averages. And this is not World War Two. The numbers are nowhere remotely comparable. And all analogies to the Holocaust are tired, overworked, boring, probably insulting, possibly true, and a major turnoff.

NED. Are they?

FELIX. Boy, I think I've found myself a real live weird one. I had no idea. (*Pause*.). Hey, I just called you weird.

NED. You are not the first.

FELIX. You've never had a lover, have you?

NED. Where did you get that from?

FELIX. Have you? Wow.

NED. I suppose you've had quite a few.

FELIX. I had a very good one for a number of years, thank you.
He was older than I was and he found someone younger.

NED. So you like them older. You looking for a father?

FELIX. No, I am not looking for a father! God, you are relentless.
And as cheery as Typhoid Mary.

> NED *comes over to* FELIX *and sits beside him. Then he leans
> over and kisses him. The kiss becomes quite intense. Then* NED
> *breaks away, jumps up, and begins to walk around nervously.*

NED. The American Jews knew exactly what was happening, but
everything was downplayed and stifled. Can you imagine how
effective it would have been if every Jew in America had
marched on Washington? Proudly! Who says I want a lover?
Huh!? I mean, why doesn't anybody believe me when I say I do
not want a lover?

FELIX. You are fucking crazy. Jews, Dachau, Final Solution –
what kind of date is this! I don't believe anyone in the whole
wide world doesn't want to be loved. Ned, you don't remember
me, do you? We've been in bed together. We made love. We
talked. We kissed. We cuddled. We made love again. I keep
waiting for you to remember, something, anything. But you
don't!

NED. How could I not remember you?

FELIX. I don't know.

NED. Maybe if I saw you naked.

FELIX. It's okay as long as we treat each other like whores. It was
at the baths a few years ago. You were busy cruising some blond
number and I stood outside your door waiting for you to come
back and when you did you gave me such an inspection up and
down you would have thought I was applying for the CIA.

NED. And then what?

FELIX. I just told you. We made love twice. I thought it was
lovely. You told me your name was Ned, that when you were a
child you read a Philip Barry play called *Holiday* where there
was a Ned, and you immediately switched from . . . Alexander?
I teased you for taking such a Wasp, up-in-Connecticut-for-the-
weekend name, and I asked what you did, and you answered
something like you'd tried a number of things, and I asked you
if that had included love, which is when you said you had to get
up early in the morning. That's when I left. But I tossed you my
favourite go-fuck-yourself yourself when you told me 'I really

am not in the market for a lover' – men do not just naturally not love – they learn not to. I am not a whore. I just sometimes make mistakes and look for love in the wrong places. And I think you're a bluffer. Your novel was all about a man desperate for love and a relationship, in a world filled with nothing but casual sex.

NED. Please don't say anymore.

FELIX. Boy, am I glad I came out in the 70s. You 60s guys are sure a mess.

NED. Do you think we could start over?

FELIX. Maybe.

Scene Five

NED's *apartment*. MICKEY, BRUCE *and* TOMMY BOATWRIGHT, *a Southerner in his late twenties, are stuffing envelopes with various inserts and then packing them into cartons. Beer and pretzels.*

MICKEY *(calling off)*. Ned, Gregory says hello and he can't believe you've turned into an activist. He says where were you fifteen years ago when we needed you.

NED *(coming in with a tray with more beer)*. You tell Gregory fifteen years ago no self-respecting faggot would have anything to do with you guys.

TOMMY. I was twelve years old.

BRUCE. We're not activists.

MICKEY. If you're not an activist, Bruce, then what are you?

BRUCE. Nothing. I'm only in this until it goes away.

MICKEY. You know, the battle against the police at Stonewall was won by transvestites. Everybody fought like hell. It's you Brooks Brothers who –

BRUCE. That's why I wasn't at Stonewall. I don't have anything in common with those guys, girls, whatever you call them. Ned, Robert Stokes has it. He called me today.

NED. At Glenn Fitzsimmons' party the other night, I saw one friend there I knew was sick, I learned about two others, and then walking home I bumped into Richie Faro, who told me he'd just been diagnosed.

MICKEY. Richie Faro?

NED. All this on Sixth Avenue between Nineteenth and Eighth Streets.

MICKEY. Richie Faro – gee, I haven't seen him since Stonewall. I think we even had a little affairlet.

BRUCE. Are you a transvestite?

MICKEY. No, but I'll fight for your right to be one.

BRUCE. I don't want to be one!

MICKEY. I'm worried this organisation might only attract white bread and middle-class. We need Blacks . . .

TOMMY. Right on!

MICKEY . . . . and . . . how do you feel about Lesbians?

BRUCE. Not very much. I mean, they're . . . something else.

MICKEY. I wonder what they're going to think about all this? If past history is any guide, there's never been much support by either half of us for the other. Tommy, are you a Lesbian?

TOMMY (*as he exits into the kitchen*). I have done and seen everything.

NED (*to* BRUCE). How are you doing?

BRUCE. I'm okay now. I forgot to thank you for sending flowers.

NED. That's okay.

BRUCE. Funny – my mother sent flowers. We've never even talked about my being gay. I told her Craig died. I guess she knew.

NED. I think mothers somehow always know. Would you like to have dinner next week, maybe see a movie?

BRUCE (*uncomfortable when* NED *makes advances*). Actually . . . it's funny . . . it happened so fast. You know Albert? I've been seeing him.

NED. That guy in the Calvin Klein ads? Great!

TOMMY *returns dragging another carton of envelopes and boxes.*

BRUCE. I don't think I like to be alone. I've always been with somebody.

MICKEY (*looking up from his list-checking*). We have to choose a President tonight, don't forget. I'm not interested. And what about a board of directors?

BRUCE *(looking at one of the flyers)*. Mickey, how did you finally decide to say it? I didn't even look.

MICKEY. I just said the best medical knowledge, which admittedly isn't very much, seems to feel that a virus has landed in our community. It could have been any community, but it landed in ours. I guess we just got in the way. Boy, are we going to have paranoia problems.

NED *(looking at a flyer)*. That's all you said?

MICKEY. See what I mean? No, I also put in the benefit dance announcement and a coupon for donations.

NED. What about the recommendations?

MICKEY. I recommended everyone should donate a million dollars. How are we going to make people realise this is not just a gay problem? If it happens to us, it can happen to anybody. I sent copies to all the gay newspapers.

BRUCE. What good will that do? Nobody reads them.

MICKEY. The *Native*'s doing a good job.

NED *(who has read the flyer and is angry)*. Mickey, I thought we talked this out on the phone. We must tell everybody what Emma wants us to tell them.

MICKEY. She wants to tell them so badly she won't lend her name as recommending it. *(To the others:)* This is what Ned wrote for me to send out. 'If this doesn't scare the shit out of you, and rouse you to action, gay men may have no future here on earth.' Neddie, I think that's a bit much.

BRUCE. You'll scare everybody to death!

NED. Shake up. What's wrong with that? This isn't something that can be force-fed gently; it won't work. Mickey neglected to read my first sentence.

MICKEY. 'It's difficult to write this without sounding alarmist or scared.' Okay, but then listen to this: 'I am sick of guys moaning that giving up careless sex until this blows over is worse than death . . . I am sick of guys who can only think of their cocks . . . I am sick of closeted gays. It's 1982 now, guys, when are you going to come out? By 1984 you could be dead.'

BRUCE. You're crazy.

NED. Am I? There are almost five hundred cases now. Okay, if we're not sending it out, I'll get the *Native* to run it.

BRUCE. But we can't tell people how to live their lives! We can't do that. And besides, the entire gay political platform is fucking. We'd get it from all sides.

NED. You make it sound like that's all that being gay means.

BRUCE. That's all it does mean!

MICKEY. It's the only thing that makes us different.

NED. I don't want to be considered different.

BRUCE. Neither do I, actually.

MICKEY. Well, I do.

BRUCE. Well, you are!

MICKEY. Unfortunately that's all it seems to have come to mean. When we started, it meant a lot more.

NED. Why is it we can only talk about our sexuality, and so relentlessly? You know, Mickey, all we've created is generations of guys who can't deal with each other as anything but erections. We can't even get a meeting with the Mayor's gay assistant!

TOMMY. I'm very interested in setting up some sort of services for the patients. We've got to start thinking about them.

BRUCE (whispering to NED). Who's he?

TOMMY. He heard about you and he found you and here he is. His name is Tommy Boatwright . . . (To NED:) Why don't you write that down? Tommy Boatwright. In real life, he's a hospital administrator. And I'm a Southern bitch.

NED. Welcome to gay politics.

BRUCE. Ned, I won't have anything to do with any organisation that tells people how to live their lives.

NED. It's not telling them. It's a recommendation.

MICKEY. With a shotgun to their heads.

BRUCE. It's interfering with their civil rights.

MICKEY. Fucking as a civil right? Don't we just wish.

TOMMY. What if we put it in the form of a recommendation from gay doctors? So that way we're just the conduit.

NED. I can't get any gay doctor to go on record and say publicly what Emma wants.

BRUCE. The fortunes they've made off our being sick, you'd think they could have warned us. (Suddenly noticing an envelope.) What the fuck is this?

MICKEY. Unh, oh!

BRUCE. Look at this! Was this your idea?

NED. I'm looking. I'm not seeing. What don't I see?

MICKEY. What we put for our return address.

NED. You mean the word 'gay' is on the envelope?

BRUCE. You're damn right. Instead of just the initials. Who did it?

NED. Well, maybe it was Pierre who designed it. Maybe it was a mistake at the printers. But it is the name we chose for this organization . . .

BRUCE. You chose. I didn't want 'gay' in it.

MICKEY. No, we all voted. That was one of those meetings when somebody actually showed up.

NED. Bruce, I think it's interesting that nobody noticed until now. You've been stuffing them all week at your apartment.

BRUCE. We can't send them out.

NED. We have to if we want anybody to come to the dance. They were late from the printers as it is.

BRUCE. We can go through and scratch out the word with a Magic Marker.

NED. Ten thousand times? Look, I feel sympathy for young guys still living at home on Long Island with their parents, but most men getting these . . . Look at you, in your case what difference does it make? You live alone, you own your own apartment, your mother lives in another State . . .

BRUCE. What about my mailman?

MICKEY *lets out a little laughing yelp, then clears his throat.*

NED. You don't expect me to take that seriously?

BRUCE. Yes, I do!

NED. What about your doorman?

BRUCE. What about him?

NED. Why don't you worry about him? All those cute little Calvin Klein numbers you parade under his nose, he thinks you're playing poker with the boys?

BRUCE. You don't have any respect for anyone who doesn't think like you do, do you?

NED. Bruce, I don't agree with you about this. I think it's imperative that we all grow up now and come out of the closet.

MICKEY. Ladies, behave! Ned, you don't think much of our sexual revolution. You say it all the time.

NED. No, I say I don't think much of promiscuity. And what's that got to do with gay envelopes?

MICKEY. But you've certainly done your share.

NED. That doesn't mean I approve of it or like myself for doing it.

MICKEY. But not all of us feel that way. And we don't like to hear the word 'promiscuous' used pejoratively.

BRUCE. Or so publicly.

NED. Where the world can hear it, Bruce?

MICKEY. Sex is liberating. It's always guys like you who've never had one who are always screaming about relationships, and monogamy and fidelity and holy matrimony. What are you, a closet straight?

NED. Mickey, more sex isn't more liberating. And having so much sex makes finding love impossible.

MICKEY. Neddie, dahling, do not put your failure to find somebody on the morality of all the rest of us.

NED. Mickey, dahling, I'm just saying what I think! It's taken me twenty years of assorted forms of therapy in various major world capitals to be able to do so without guilt, fear, or giving a fuck if anybody likes it or not.

TOMMY. I'll buy that!

NED. Thank you.

BRUCE. But not everyone's so free to say what they think!

MICKEY. Or able to afford so much therapy. Although God knows I need it. *(Looking at his watch.)* Look, it's late, and we haven't elected our President. Ned, I think it should be . . . Bruce. Everybody knows him and likes him and . . .I mean, everybody expects you to –

NED. You mean he's popular and everybody's afraid of me.

MICKEY. Yes.

TOMMY. No.

MICKEY. No.

TOMMY. No, what it means is that you have a certain kind of energy that's definitely needed, but Bruce has a . . . presence that might bring people together in a way you can't.

NED. What's that mean?

TOMMY. It means he's gorgeous – and all the kids on Christopher Street and Fire Island will feel a bit more comfortable following him.

NED. Just like high school.

TOMMY AND MICKEY. Yes

NED. Follow him where?

TOMMY *(putting his arm around him)*. Well, honey, why don't we have a little dinner and I'll tell you all about it – and more.

NED. Uhn, thanks, I'm busy.

TOMMY. Forever? Well, that's too bad. I wanted to try my hand at smoothing out your rough edges.

MICKEY. Good luck.

NED *(to* BRUCE). Well, it looks like you're the President.

BRUCE. I don't think I want this.

NED. Oh, come on, you're gorgeous – and we're all going to follow you.

BRUCE. Fuck you. I accept.

NED. Well, fuck you, congratulations.

TOMMY. There are going to be a lot of scared people out there needing someplace to call for information. I'd be interested in starting some sort of telephone hotline.

BRUCE *(his first decision in office)*. Unh . . . sure. Just prepare a detailed budget and let me see it before you make any commitments.

MICKEY *(to* NED). Don't you feel in safe hands already?

TOMMY (to BRUCE). What is it you do for a living, if I may ask?

BRUCE. I'm a vice-president of Citibank.

TOMMY. That's nothing to be shy about, sugar. You invented the Cash Machine. *(Picking up an envelope.)* So, are we mailing these out or what?

BRUCE. What do you think?

TOMMY. I'll bet nobody even notices.

BRUCE. Oh, there will be some who notice. Okay.

TOMMY. Okay? Okay! Our first adult compromise. Thank y'all for your co-operation.

FELIX, *carrying a shopping bag, lets himself in with his own key.* NED *goes to greet him.*

NED. Everybody, this is Felix. Bruce, Tommy, Mickey. Bruce just got elected President.

FELIX. My condolences. Don't let me interrupt. Anybody want any Balducci gourmet ice cream – it's eighteen bucks a pint?

NED *and* FELIX *go into the kitchen.*

MICKEY. It looks like Neddie's found a boyfriend.

BRUCE. Thank God, now maybe he'll leave me alone.

TOMMY. Shit, he's got his own key. It looks like I signed on too late.

BRUCE. I worry about Ned. I mean, I like him a lot but, well, not everyone agrees with him and . . . his style is so . . . confrontative.

MICKEY. There's no such word.

BRUCE. You know what I mean. We may get into a lot of trouble with Ned.

TOMMY. Honey, he looks like a pretty good catch to me. We could get into a lot of trouble without him.

NED *and* FELIX *come back.* FELIX *cleans up after the guys.*

MICKEY. I'm going home. My Gregory, he burns dinner every night, and when I'm late, he blames me.

BRUCE *(to* NED*).* My boss doesn't know and he hates gays. He keeps telling me fag jokes and I keep laughing at them.

NED. Citibank won't fire you for being gay. And if they did, we could make such a stink that every gay customer in New York would leave them. Come on, Bruce – you used to be a fucking Green Beret!

TOMMY. Goodness!

BRUCE. But I love my job. I supervise a couple thousand people all over the country and my investments are up to twenty million now.

MICKEY. I'm leaving. *(He hefts a carton and starts out.)*

BRUCE. Wait, I'm coming. *(To* NED*:)* I just think we have to stay out of anything political.

FELIX *goes back into the kitchen.*

NED. And I think it's going to be impossible to pass along any information or recommendation that isn't going to be considered political by somebody.

TOMMY. And I think this is not an argument you two boys are going to settle tonight.

BRUCE *starts out and as he passes* NED, NED *stops and*

kisses him goodbye on the mouth. BRUCE *picks up a big carton and heads out.*

(TOMMY *has waited impatiently for* BRUCE *to leave so he can be alone with* NED.) I just wanted to tell you I really admire your writing . . . and your passion . . . (As FELIX *re-enters from the kitchen,* TOMMY *drops his flirtatious tone.*) . . . and what you've been saying and doing, and it's because of you I'm here. *(To* FELIX:) Take care this good man doesn't burn out. Good night. *(He leaves.)*

NED. We just elected a president who's in the closet. I lost every argument. And I'm the only screamer among them. Oh, I forgot to tell them – I'm getting us something on the local news.

FELIX. Which channel?

NED. It's not TV, it's radio . . . It's a start.

FELIX. Ned, I think you should have been President.

NED. I didn't really want it. I've never been any good playing on a team. I like stirring things up on my own. Bruce will be a good president. I'll shape him up. Where's the ice cream? Do you think I'm crazy?

FELIX. I certainly do. That's why I'm here.

NED. I'm so glad.

FELIX. That I'm here?

NED. That you think I'm crazy.

They kiss.

Scene Six

BEN's *office. In a corner is a large model of the new house under a cloth cover.*

BEN. You got your free legal work from my firm; now I'm not going to be on your board of directors, too.

NED. I got our free legal work from your firm by going to Norman and he said, 'Of course, no problem.' I asked him, 'Don't you have to put it before your committee?' And he said, 'Nah, I'll just tell them we're going to do it.'

BEN. Well . . . you got it.

NED. All I'm asking for is the use of your name. You don't have to do a thing. This is an honorary board. For the stationery.

BEN. Ned, come on – it's your cause, not mine. I don't ask you to help me with the Larchmont school board, do I?

NED. But I would if you asked me.

BEN. But I don't.

NED. Would you be more interested if you thought this was a straight disease?

BEN. It has nothing to do with your being gay.

NED. Of course it has. What else has it got to do with?

BEN. I've got other things to do.

NED. But I'm telling you you don't have to do a thing!

BEN. The answer is 'No'.

NED. It's impossible to get this epidemic taken seriously. I wrote a letter to the gay newspaper and some guy wrote in 'Oh there goes Ned Weeks again; he wants us all to die so he can say "I told you so."'

BEN. He sounds like a crazy.

NED. It kept me up all night.

BEN. Then you're crazy, too.

NED. I ran into an old friend I hadn't seen in years in the subway, and I said, 'Hello, how are you?' He started screaming, 'You're giving away all our secrets, you're painting us as sick, you're destroying homosexuality' – and then he tried to slug me. Right there in the subway. Under Bloomingdale's .

BEN. Another crazy.

NED. We did raise $50,000 at our dance last week. That's more money than any gay organisation has ever raised at one time in this city before.

BEN. That's wonderful, Ned. So you must be beginning to do something right.

NED. And I made a speech appealing for volunteers and we got over a hundred people to sign up, including a few women. And I've got us on Donahue. I'm going to be on Donahue with a doctor and a patient.

BEN. Don't tell your mother.

NED. Why not?

BEN. She's afraid someone is going to shoot you.

BEN *rolls the model house stage centre and pulls off the cover.*

NED. Excuse me – is this a bad time? You seem preoccupied.

BEN. Do I? I'm sorry. A morning with the architect is enough to shake me up a little bit. It's going to cost more than I thought.

NED. More?

BEN. Twice as much.

NED. Two million?

BEN. I can handle it.

NED. You can? That's very nice. You know, Ben, one of these days I'll make you agree that over twenty million men and women are not all here on this earth because of something requiring the services of a psychiatrist.

BEN. Oh, it's up to twenty million now, is it? Every time we have this discussion you up the ante.

NED. We haven't had this discussion in years, Ben. And we grow, just like everybody else.

BEN. Look, I try to understand. I read stuff.

Picking up a copy of Newsweek, *with 'Gay America' on the cover.*

I open magazines and I see pictures of you guys in leather and chains and whips and black masks, with captions saying this is a social worker, this is a computer analyst, this is a schoolteacher – and I say to myself, 'This isn't Ned'.

NED. No, it isn't. It isn't most of us. You know the media always dramatises the most extreme. Do you think we all wear dresses, too?

BEN. Don't you?

NED. Me, personally? No, I do not.

BEN. But then you tell me how you go to the bathhouses and fuck blindly, and to me that's not so different from this. You guys don't seem to understand why there are rules, and regulations, guidelines, responsibilities. You guys have a dreadful image problem.

NED. I know that! That's what has to be changed. That's why it's so important to have people like you supporting us. You're a respected person. You already have your dignity.

BEN. We better decide where we're going to eat lunch and get out of here. I have an important meeting.

NED. Do you? How important? I've asked for your support.

BEN. In every area I consider important you have my support.

NED. In some place deep inside of you you still think I'm sick. Isn't that right? Okay. Define it for me. What do you mean by 'sick'? Sick unhealthy? Sick perverted? Sick I'll get over it? Sick to be locked up?

BEN. I think you've adjusted to life quite well.

NED. All things considered?

BEN *nods.*

In the only area I consider important I don't have your support at all. The single-minded determination of all you people to forever see us as sick helps keep us sick.

BEN. I saw how unhappy you were!

NED. So were you! You wound up going to shrinks, too. We grew up side by side. We both felt pretty much the same about Mom and Pop. I refuse to accept for one more second that I was damaged by our childhood while you were not.

BEN. But we all don't react the same way to the same thing.

NED. That's right. So I became a writer and you became a lawyer. I'll agree to the fact that I have any number of awful character traits. But not to the fact that whatever they did to us as kids automatically made me sick and gay while you stayed straight and healthy.

BEN. Well, that's the difference of opinion we have over theory.

NED. But your theory turns me into a man from Mars. My theory doesn't do that to you.

BEN. Are you suggesting it was wrong of me to send you into therapy so young? I didn't think you'd stay in it forever.

NED. I didn't think I'd done anything wrong until you sent me into it. Ben, you know you mean more to me than anyone else in the world; you always have. Although I think I've finally found someone I like . . . Don't you understand?

BEN. No, I don't understand.

NED. You've got to say it. I'm the same as you. Just say it. Say it !

BEN. No, you're not. I can't say it.

NED *(he is heartbroken)*. Every time I lose this fight it hurts more. I don't want to have lunch. I'll see you. *(He starts out.)*

BEN. Come on, lemon, I still love you. Sarah loves you. Our children. Our cat. Our dog . . .

NED. You think this is a joke!

BEN *(angry)*. You have my love and you have my legal advice and my financial supervision. I can't give you the courage to stand up and say to me that you don't give a good healthy fuck what I think. Please stop trying to wring some admission of guilt out of me. I am truly happy that you've met someone. It's about time. And I'm sorry your friends are dying . . .

NED. If you're so sorry, join our honorary board and say you're sorry out loud!

BEN. My agreeing you were born just like I was born is not going to help save your dying friends.

NED. Funny – that's exactly what I think will help save my dying friends.

BEN. Ned – you can be gay and you can be proud no matter what I think. Everybody is oppressed by somebody else in some form or another. Some of us learn how to fight back, with or without the help of others, despite their opinions, even those closest to us. And judging from this mess your friends are in, it's imperative that you stand up and fight to be prouder than ever.

NED. Can't you see that I'm trying to do that? Can't your perverse ego proclaiming its superiority see that I'm trying to be proud? You can only find room to call yourself normal.

BEN. You make me sound like I'm the enemy.

NED. I'm beginning to think that you and your straight world are our enemy. I'm trying to understand why nobody wants to hear we're dying, why nobody wants to help, why my own brother doesn't want to help. Two million dollars – for a house! We can't even get twenty-nine cents from the city. You still think I'm sick, and I simply cannot allow that any longer. I am furious with you, and with myself and with every goddamned doctor who ever told me I'm sick and interfered with my loving a man. I will not speak to you again until you accept me as your equal. Your healthy equal. Your brother. (*He runs out.*)

Scene Seven

NED's *apartment. NED and FELIX are spread out with comforters, pillows, books, paper, and pencils. NED eats from a container of ice cream.*

NED. Have I ever been with a woman? Once. When I was 32.

FELIX. All you ever eat is desserts.

NED. Sugar is the most important thing in life. All the rest is just to stay alive.

FELIX. Who was she?

NED. Her name, believe it or not, was Delilah, and she was, wouldn't you know it, a stand-in on one of my movies. She was a very nice woman. I asked a straight friend to explain to me where everything was, I thought I knew, but I had to be sure, just in case, and I had her over to dinner and afterward . . . at what I deemed to be the most suitable moment, because I'd been communicating to it down there: 'are you ready? are you absolutely certain you're ready?' and it seemed it was ready, I picked her up in my arms, very Rhett Butler, and carried her up to my bedroom, where . . . I couldn't get it up.

FELIX. How I remember.

NED. You too?

FELIX *nods*.

But in the middle of the night I woke up with this huge erection. God knows who or what I'd been dreaming about but I quickly shook her awake, shouting 'please stick it in for me, Delilah,' I was afraid it would go down while I was hunting for the proper place . . . and she did, and I did, and it did, and we did . . . and the very next day, I couldn't wait to get there, he lived in a place called the Vale of Health – I was positively under the spell of this High Freudian on Hampstead Heath, they don't ever talk to you that's how you know you're expected to make the old college try . . . I rushed into Dr Gillespie, I clapped the great stone face on his shoulder, and 1, who have been fucking with fellows since 8th Grade, hysterically proclaimed 'I am no longer a virgin!'

They kiss.

Tell me about yours.

FELIX. I was married.

NED. You never told me that.

FELIX. We were childhood sweethearts. I found out I was gay after we got married. And after we had a son. No, that isn't true – I think I always knew but I wouldn't admit it to myself. She was really angry – said I'd been unfair to her . . . which I had been. Anyway, she's remarried and he's rich and they live in Honolulu and would prefer . . . I'm not allowed to see my boy. I guess one reason I don't broadcast is because of him.

NED. You can't see your own son? Didn't you fight back? But that means you're ashamed. So he will be too.

FELIX. That's why I didn't tell you. Ned, don't. Not tonight. Okay?

NED. Okay.

FELIX. You love it.

NED. What?

FELIX. All the fighting.

NED. I love it?

> FELIX *nods*.

> *Moi?*

FELIX *nods*.

FELIX. Yes, you do, and you're having a wonderful time.

NED *(touching FELIX's face)*. Yes, I am. If I had it, would you leave me?

FELIX. I . . . don't know. Would you, if I did?

NED. No.

FELIX. How do you know?

NED. I just know. You had to have had my mother. She was a dedicated full-time social worker for the Red Cross. She was always getting an award for being best bloodcatcher or something. I don't think I'm programmed any other way. Emerick Nolan died.

FELIX *(shivering a little)*. I know. He gave me my first job at the *Washington Post*.

> *The phone rings.* NED *answers it.*

NED. Hello? Hold on.

> *He stands up and goes to a pile of papers, finds what he wants, and reads into the phone.*

> 'It is no secret that I consider our Mayor to be, along with the *Times,* the biggest enemy gay men and women must contend with in New York. Until the day I die I will never forgive this newspaper and this Mayor for ignoring this epidemic which is killing so many of my friends.' All right, here's the end: 'And every gay man who is unable to come forward now and fight to save his own life is truly helping to kill the rest of us. How many of us have to die before you get scared off your ass and into action?' Thank *you. (He hangs up.)* I hear it's becoming known as the Ned Weeks School of Outrage.

FELIX. All those shrinks – they must have done something right.

NED. Dr Ritvo, Dr Malev, Dr Gillespie, Dr Greenacre, Dr Harkavy, Dr Klagsbrun, Dr Donadello, Dr Levy . . . did it have to take so long?

FELIX. You think it's them, do you? I did speak to one of our science reporters.

NED. Felix, good for you ! What did he say?

FELIX. It turns out he's gay too. And afraid they'll find out. Don't yell at me! I tried.

NED. At the rate I'm going no one in this city will be talking to me in about three more weeks. I had another fight with Bruce today. I slammed the phone down on him. I don't think people like me work at Citibank.

FELIX. Why can't you see what an ordinary guy Bruce is? I know you think he has hidden qualities, if you just give him plant food he'll grow into the fighter you are. He can't. All he's got is a lot of good looking Pendleton shirts.

NED. I know there are better ways to handle him. I just can't seem to. This epidemic is killing friendships, too. I can't even talk to my own brother. Why doesn't he call me?

FELIX. There's the phone.

NED. Why do I always have to do the running back?

FELIX. What was the fight about?

NED. Which fight?

FELIX. Bruce.

NED. Pick a subject.

FELIX. How many do you know now?

NED (*consults a green notebook*). Forty . . . dead. That's too many for one person to know. Bruce is really paranoid: now his lover, Albert, isn't feeling well. Bruce is afraid he's giving it to everyone.

FELIX. Maybe it isn't paranoia. Maybe what we do with our lovers is what we should be thinking about most of all. Then why do you yell at him?

NED. He doesn't support me. The whole board yelled at me last night for two hours. We have 600 volunteers now. I've got us mentioned in *Time, Newsweek,* the evening news on all three networks, both local and national, English and French and Canadian and Australian TV, all the New York papers except the *Times*, I'm really orchestrating this well, I just know I am .

FELIX. You are. What's bugging them?

NED (*counting on his fingers*). They think I'm creating a panic, I'm using it to make myself into a celebrity – not one of them will appear on TV or agree to be interviewed when I ask them, so I do it all by default, so now I'm accused of being self-serving, as if it's fun getting slugged in the subway . . . I'm making enemies, I need to be loved, I enjoy playing the victim, I'm creating homophobia . . . Dr . . . I can't remember which one, said, it would finally happen – someone I couldn't scare away would finally show up.

FELIX. At the baths, why didn't you tell me you were a writer?

NED. Why didn't you tell me you worked for the *Times?* That I would have remembered.

FELIX. If I had told you what I did, would you have seen me again?

NED. Absolutely.

FELIX. You slut!

NED. Felix, we weren't ready then.

FELIX. It's sad how much time we lost.

NED. Don't say that. We've got . . . If we're typical faggots . . . if we're real lucky . . . I give us three more weeks.

FELIX. Don't say that.

NED. You're right.

FELIX. What happens when people can't be as strong as you want them to be?

NED. Felix, weakness terrifies me. It scares the shit out of me. My dad was weak and I'm afraid I'll be like him. His life didn't stand for anything and then it was over. So I fight. Constantly. And if I can do it, I can't understand why everybody else can't do it, too . . . Okay?

FELIX. Okay.

FELIX *pulls off one of his socks and shows* NED *that he has a purple spot on the sole of his foot.*

. . . It keeps getting bigger and bigger, Neddie, and it doesn't go away.

End of Act One.

ACT TWO

Scene Eight

EMMA's *apartment*. EMMA *and* NED *are having brunch. She uses a non-motorized wheelchair.*

NED. All we do in this country is eat. I can't find your jam. I should have brought some jam.

EMMA. You brought enough. I'll eat for a week.

NED. You look very pretty.

EMMA. Thank you.

NED. You have a very nice apartment.

EMMA. I forgot you've never been here.

NED. All our late night phone conversations, it's like I have. Where's your cat?

EMMA. Under my bed. She's afraid of you.

NED. She must read the *Native*. Do you think being Jewish makes you always hungry?

EMMA. I'm not Jewish.

NED. You're not?

EMMA. I'm German.

NED. Everyone thinks you're Jewish.

EMMA. I know. In medicine that helps.

NED. The joke around is that if this were happening to Jews there'd be a hospital already. How many of us do you think already have the virus in our system?

EMMA. In this city – easily over half of all gay men.

NED. So we're walking time bombs, waiting for whatever it is that sets us off . . .

EMMA. Yes. And before a vaccine can be discovered almost every gay man will have been exposed. Ned, your organisation is worthless! I went up and down Christopher Street last night and all I saw was guys going in the bars alone and coming out with somebody. And outside the baths, all I saw was lines of guys going in. And what is this stupid publication you finally put out? *(She holds up a pamphlet.)* After all we've talked about? You leave too much margin for intelligence. Why aren't you telling them, bluntly, stop! Every day you don't tell them, more people infect each other.

NED. Don't yell at me. I'm on your side.

EMMA. Don't be on my side! I don't need you on my side. Make your side shape up. I've seen 238 cases: me: one doctor. You make it sound like there's nothing worse going around than measles.

NED. They wouldn't print what I wrote. Again.

EMMA. What do you mean 'They'? Who's they? I thought you and Bruce were the leaders.

NED. Now we've got a Board. You need a Board of Directors when you become tax-exempt. It was hard finding anyone to serve on it at all! I called every prominent gay man I could get to. Guys who've made millions out of us . . . fashion, rock, pop, movies, real estate, you name it. Forget it! Finally, what we put together turns out to be a bunch of guys as conservative as Bruce. And every time Bruce doesn't agree with me, he puts it to a Board vote.

EMMA. And you lose.

NED *(nods)*. Bruce is in the closet. Mickey works for the Health Department. He starts shaking every time I criticise them. Richard, Dick and Lennie owe their jobs somehow to the Mayor; Dan is a schoolteacher; we're not allowed to say his last name out loud; the rest are just a bunch of disco dumbies. I warned you this was not a community that has its best interests at heart.

EMMA. But this is death.

NED. And the Board doesn't want any sex recommendations at all. No passing along any information that isn't 100 per cent certain –

EMMA. You must tell them that's wrong! Nothing is a hundred per cent certain in science, so you won't be saying anything.

NED. I think that's the general idea.

EMMA. Then why did you bother to start an organisation at all?

NED. Now they've decided they only want to take care of patients – crisis counselling, support groups, home attendants . . . I know that's important, too. But I thought I was starting with a bunch of Ralph Naders and Green Berets, and the first instant they have to take a stand on a political issue and fight, almost in front of my eyes they turn into a bunch of nurses' aides.

EMMA. You've got to warn the living, protect the healthy, help them keep on living. I'll take care of the dying.

NED. They keep yelling at me that I can't expect an entire world to suddenly stop making love.

EMMA. I don't consider going to the baths and promiscuous sex making love. I consider it the equivalent of eating junk food, and you can lay off it for a while. And, yes, I do expect it, and you get them to come sit in my office any day of the week and they'd expect it, too. Get a VCR, rent a porn film, and use your hands! You spend so many years working so hard, getting an education to make people well and I can't seem to . . .

NED. Everybody learns a little bit more each day.

EMMA. I'm not learning a little bit more each day. And damn it, I'm smart. Smart as they come.

NED. Why are you yelling at me for what I'm not doing? What the fuck is your side doing? Where's the goddamned American Medical Association in all of this? The government has not started one single test tube of research. Where's the Board of Directors of your very own hospital? You have so many patients you haven't got rooms for them, and you've got to make Felix well . . . So what am I yelling at you for?

EMMA. Who's Felix? Who is Felix?

NED. I introduced you to him at that Health Forum you spoke at.

EMMA. You've taken a lover?

NED. We live together. Emma, I've never been so much in love in my life. I've never been in love. Late Friday night he showed me this purple spot on the bottom of his foot. Maybe it isn't it. Maybe it's some sort of something else. It could be, couldn't it? Can you see him tomorrow? I know you're booked up for weeks. But could you?

EMMA. Tell him to call me first thing tomorrow. Seven-thirty. I'll fit him in.

NED. Thank you.

EMMA. God damn you!

NED. I know I should have told you.

EMMA. What's done is done.

NED. What are we supposed to do – be with nobody ever? Well, it's not as easy as you might think.

She wheels herself directly in front of him.

Oh, Emma, I'm so sorry. Do you mind if I ask you . . . ?

EMMA. I had polio when I was a kid. I caught it three months before the Salk vaccine was announced.

NED. Were you in an iron lung?

EMMA. I was.

NED. How did you go to school?

EMMA. School came to me. I was only in an iron lung for a couple of years. Then I had to stay in bed for a few years after that. I was connected to my classroom by a little loudspeaker that was on my bedstand. I could hear everything and I'd press a button when I wanted to speak. This is outside Boston, I'm a Yankee. Every few months a couple of kids would be required to come visit me; and we'd say hello and then not know what to say to each other after that. 'Oh I recognise you by your voice,' 'Oh me too!' And that was about it. They were terrified of me. Still are. I scare the shit out of people. The holy terror in the wheelchair.

NED. I think I'm beginning to scare people too.

EMMA. Learn how to use it. It can be very useful. Don't need everybody's love and approval.

NED. You stayed in bed all the way through school?

EMMA. By college I had my first braces and I could walk a little. Then I got into wheelchairs when I went to medical school and now I'm lazy. I graduated from college and from medical school first in my class. I don't walk so good any more, but that's just because I'm too busy to practise.

NED. You must practise!

EMMA. One of these days I'll start again.

NED. Right now! Come on, right now. No, I mean it. Come on. *(He stands in front of her.)*

EMMA. Okay. You asked for it.

NED. May I have this dance?

She pulls herself up and out of the chair. She hobbles forward clumsily, then better, putting her feet in front of each other more or less satisfactorily but then she makes a mis-step and tries to get her balance before falling into his arms. The intimacy of this moment is thrilling to him. They are each holding tightly to the other.

NED. I'm afraid to leave him alone now. I'm afraid to be with

him. I'm afraid to be without him. I'm afraid the cure won't
come in time. I'm afraid my anger is just making everyone
angry – at me. I'm a terrible leader and a useless lover and . . .

EMMA. And a lousy dancer. Put me back.

NED *(as he helps her back into her wheelchair)*. You know you're
guaranteed to not let anyone have any self-pity . . . Maybe he
doesn't have it. Maybe I'm over-reacting. There's so much
death around.

EMMA. Polio is a virus too. Nobody gets polio any more.

He hugs her and leaves. EMMA is alone.

Scene Nine

*A meeting room in City Hall. It's in a basement, windowless,
dusty, a room that's hardly ever used. NED and BRUCE wait
impatiently: they have been fighting. BRUCE wears a suit, having
come from his office, with his attaché case. Both wear overcoats.*

NED. How dare they do this to us?

BRUCE. It's one-thirty. Maybe he's not going to show up. Why
don't we just leave?

NED. Keeping us down here in some basement room that hasn't
been used in years. What contempt!

BRUCE. I'm sorry I let you talk me into coming here. It's not the
city's responsibility to take care of us. That's why New York
went broke.

NED. What we're asking for doesn't cost the city a dime: let us
meet with the Mayor; let him put pressure on Washington for
money for research; have him get the *Times* to write about us.

BRUCE. The Mayor's not going to help. Besides, if we get too
political, we'll lose our tax-exempt status. That's what the
lawyer in your brother's office said.

NED. You don't think the American Cancer Society, the Salvation
Army, any charity you can think of, isn't somehow political,
isn't putting pressure on somebody somewhere? The Catholic
Church? We should be riding herd on the CDC in Atlanta –
they deny it's happening in straight people, when it is. We
could organise boycotts . . .

BRUCE. Boycotts! What in the world is there to boycott?

NED. Have you been following this Tylenol scare? In three months there have been seven deaths, and the *Times* has written fifty-four articles. The month of October alone they ran one article every single day. Four of them were on the front page. For us – in seventeen months they've written seven puny inside articles. And we have a thousand cases!

BRUCE. So?

NED. So the *Times* won't write about us, why should we read it?

BRUCE. I read it every morning. The next thing you'll say is we should stop shopping at Bloomingdale's.

NED. We should picket the White House!

BRUCE. Brilliant.

NED. Don't you have any vision of what we could become? A powerful national organisation effecting change! Bruce, you must have been a fighter once. When you were a Green Beret, did you kill people?

BRUCE. A couple of times.

NED. Did you like being a soldier?

BRUCE. I loved it.

NED. Then why did you quit?

BRUCE. I didn't quit. I just don't like being earmarked gay.

NED. Bruce, what are you doing in this organisation?

BRUCE. There are a lot of sick people out there that need our help.

NED. There are going to be a lot more sick people out there if we don't get our act together. Did you give up combat completely.

BRUCE. Don't you fucking talk to me about combat! I just fight different from you.

NED. I haven't seen your way yet.

BRUCE. Oh, you haven't? Where have you been?

NED. Bruce, Albert may be dying. Why doesn't that alone make you want to fight harder?

BRUCE. Get off my back!

NED. Get off your ass!

TOMMY *enters*.

TOMMY. Wonderful – we finally get a meeting with the Mayor's assistant and you two are having another fight.

BRUCE. I didn't have the fight, he had the fight. It's always Ned who has the fight.

TOMMY. Where the hell are we? What kind of tomb is this they put us in? Don't they want us to be seen above ground? Where is he? I'm an hour late.

NED. An hour and a half. And where's Mickey?

TOMMY. Not with me, lambchop. I've been up at Bellevue. I put a sweet dying child together with his momma. They hadn't seen each other for fifteen years and he'd never told her he was gay, so he didn't want to see her now. He's been refusing to see her for weeks and he was furious with me when I waltzed in with her and . . . It was a real weeper, Momma holding her son, and he's dead now. There are going to be a lot of mommas flying into town not understanding why their sons have suddenly upped and died from 'pneumonia'. You two've been barking at each other for an hour and a half? My, my.

BRUCE. Tommy, he makes me so mad.

NED. CBS called. They want our President to go on Dan Rather. He won't do it. They don't want anybody else.

BRUCE. I can't go on national television!

NED. Then you shouldn't be our President! Tommy, look at that. Imagine what a fantastic impression he would make on the whole country, speaking out for something gay. You're the kind of role model we need, not those drag queens from San Francisco who shove their faces in front of every camera they see.

BRUCE. You want to pay me my salary and my pension and my health insurance, I'll go on TV.

TOMMY. Both of you, stop it. Can't you see we need both your points of view? Ned plays the bad cop and Bruce plays the good cop; every successful corporation works that way. You're both our leaders and we need you both desperately.

NED. Tommy, how is not going on national TV playing good cop?

MICKEY *enters*.

MICKEY. I couldn't get out of work. I was afraid you'd be finished by now.

BRUCE (*to* MICKEY). Did you see his latest *Native* article?

MICKEY. Another one?

NED. What's so awful about what I said? It's the truth.

BRUCE. But it's how you say it!

MICKEY. What'd you say?

NED. I said we're all cowards! I said rich gays will give thousands
   to straight charities before they'll give us a dime. I said it is
   appalling that some twenty million men and women don't have
   one single lobbyist in Washington. How do we expect to
   achieve anything, ever, at all, by immaculate conception? I said
   the gay leaders who created this sexual-liberation philosophy in
   the first place have been the death of us. Mickey, why didn't
   you guys fight for the right to get married instead of the right to
   legitimise promiscuity?

MICKEY. We did!

TOMMY. I get your drift.

MICKEY. Sure you didn't leave anybody out?

NED. I said it's all our fault, every one of us . . .

   HIRAM KEEBLER, *the Mayor's assistant, enters, and* NED
   carries on without a break.

   . . . and you are an hour and forty-five minutes late, so why'd
   you bother to come at all?

BRUCE. Ned!

HIRAM. I presume I am at last having the pleasure of meeting Mr
   Weeks' lilting telephone voice face to face. *(Shaking hands all
   around.)* I'm truly sorry I'm late.

MICKEY *(shaking hands)*. Michael Marcus.

HIRAM. I'm Hiram Keebler.

TOMMY. Are you related to the folks who make the crackers?
   Tommy Boatwright.

BRUCE. Bruce Niles.

HIRAM. The Mayor wants you to know how much he cares and
   how impressed he is with your superb efforts to shoulder your
   own responsibility.

BRUCE. Thank you.

NED. Our responsibility? Everything we're doing is stuff you
   should be doing. And we need help.

TOMMY. What Mr Weeks is trying to say, sir, is that, well, we are
   truly swamped. We're now fielding over five hundred calls a
   week on our emergency hot line, people everywhere are
   desperate for information, which, quite frankly, the city should
   be providing, but isn't. We're visiting over one hundred
   patients each week in hospitals and homes and . . .

BRUCE. Sir, one thing you could help us with is office space. We're presently in one small room, and at least one hundred people come in and out every day and . . . no one will rent to us because of what we do and who we are.

HIRAM. That's illegal discrimination.

TOMMY. We believe we know that to be true, sir.

MICKEY (nervously speaking up). Mr Keebler, sir, it is not illegal to discriminate against homosexuals.

NED. We have been trying to see the Mayor for fourteen months. It has taken us one year just to get this meeting with you and you are an hour and forty-five minutes late. Have you told the Mayor there's an epidemic going on?

HIRAM. I can't tell him that!

NED. Why not?

HIRAM. Because it isn't true.

BRUCE. Yes, sir, it is.

HIRAM. Who said so?

TOMMY. The Government.

HIRAM. Which government? Our government?

NED. No ! Russia's government !

HIRAM. Since when?

MICKEY. The Center for Disease Control in Atlanta declared it.

TOMMY. Seventeen months ago.

NED. How could you not know that?

HIRAM. Well, you can't expect us to concern ourselves with every little outbreak those boys come up with. And could you please reduce the level of your hysteria?

NED. Certainly. San Francisco, L.A., Miami, Boston, Chicago, Washington, Denver, Houston, Seattle, Dallas – all now report cases. It's cropping up in Paris, London, Germany, Canada. But New York City, our home, the city you are pledged to protect, has over half of everything: half the one thousand cases, half the dead. Two hundred and fifty-six dead. And I know forty of them. And I don't want to know any more. And you can't not know any of this! Now – when can we see the Mayor? Fourteen months is a long time to be out to lunch!

HIRAM. Now wait a minute!

NED. No, you wait a minute. We can't. Time is not on our side. If

you won't take word to the Mayor, what do we do? How do we
get it to him? Hire a hunky hustler and send him up to Gracie
Mansion with our plea tattooed on his cock?

HIRAM. The Mayor is not gay!

TOMMY. Oh, come on, Blanche!

BRUCE. Tommy!

HIRAM. Now you listen to me! Of course we're aware of those
figures. And before you open your big mouth again, I would
like to offer you a little piece of advice. Bad-mouthing the
Mayor is the best way I know to not get his attention.

NED. We're not getting it now, so what have we got to lose?

BRUCE. Ned!

NED. Bruce, you just heard him. Hiram here just said they're
aware of the figures. And they're still not doing anything. I was
worried before that they were just stupid and blind. Great! Now
we get to worry about them being repressive and downright
dangerous.

BRUCE. Ned! I'm sorry, sir, but we've been under a great deal of
strain.

NED (to BRUCE). Don't you ever apologise for me again. (To
HIRAM.) How dare you choose who will live and who will die!

HIRAM. Now listen: don't you think I want to help you?
(Confidentially) I have a friend who's dying from this in VA
Hospital right this very minute.

NED. Then why . . . ?

HIRAM. Because it's tricky, can't you see that? It's very tricky.

NED. Tricky, shit! There are a million gay people in New York. A
million and one, counting you. That's a lot of votes. Our
organisation started with six men. We now have over six
hundred active volunteers and a mailing list of ten thousand.

HIRAM. Six hundred? You think the Mayor worries about six
hundred? A fire goes out in a school furnace on the West Side
between Seventy-Second and Ninety-Sixth streets, I get three
thousand phone calls. In one day! You know what I'm talking
about?

NED. Yes?

HIRAM. If so many of you are so upset about what's happening,
why do I only hear from this loudmouth?

NED. That's a very good question.

HIRAM. Okay – there are half a million gay men in our area. Five hundred and nine cases doesn't seem so high, considering how many of us – I mean, of you! – there are.

NED. This is bullshit!

BRUCE. Ned! Let me take it. Sir –

HIRAM. Hiram, please. You are?

BRUCE. I'm Bruce Niles. I'm the President.

HIRAM. You're the President? What does that make Mr Weeks here?

BRUCE. He's one of the founders.

NED. But we work together jointly.

HIRAM. Oh, you do?

NED. Yes, we do.

HIRAM. Carry on, Mr Niles.

BRUCE. Look, we realise things are tricky, but –

HIRAM (*cutting him off*). Yes, it is. And the Mayor feels there is no need to declare any kind of emergency. That only gets people excited. And we simply can't give you office space. We're not in the free-giveaway business.

BRUCE. We don't want it for free. We will pay for it.

HIRAM. I repeat, I think – that is, the Mayor thinks you guys are over-reacting.

NED. You tell the Mayor that I think he's a selfish heartless, son of a bitch!

HIRAM. You are now heading for real trouble! Do you think you can barge in here and call us names? (*To* MICKEY:) You are Michael L. Marcus. You hold an unsecured job with the City Department of Health. I'd watch my step if I were you. You got yourself quite a handful here. You might consider putting him in a cage in the zoo. That I think I can arrange with the Mayor. I'd watch out for my friends here if I were you. The Mayor won't have it *! (He goes.)*

MICKEY. I don't believe this just happened.

NED. Mickey, I'm on the *Today Show* tomorrow and I'm going to say the Mayor is threatening your job if we don't shut up.

MICKEY. The *Today Show!* You're going to do what?!

BRUCE. You can't do that!

NED. Of course I can: he just did.

BRUCE. God damn it, Ned!

NED. We're being treated like shit. *(He yells after them as they pick up their things and leave.)* And we're allowing it. And until we force them to treat us otherwise, we get exactly what we deserve. Politicians understand only one thing – pressure! You heard him – him and his three thousand West Side phone calls. We're not yelling loud enough! Bruce, for a Green Beret, you're an awful sissy! *(He is all alone.)*

Scene Ten

EMMA's *office.* FELIX *sits on the examining table, wearing a white hospital gown.* EMMA *sits facing him.*

FELIX. So it is . . . it.

EMMA. Yes.

FELIX. There's not a little bit of doubt in your mind? You don't want to call in Christian Barnard?

EMMA. I'm sorry. I still don't know how to tell people. They don't teach acting in medical school.

FELIX. Aren't you worried about contagion? I mean, I assume I am about to become a leper.

EMMA. Well, I'm still here.

FELIX. Do you think they'll find a cure before I . . . How strange that sounds when you say it out loud for the first time.

EMMA. We're trying. But we're poor. Uncle Sam is the only place these days that can afford the kind of research that's needed, and so far we've not even had the courtesy of a reply from our numerous requests to him. You guys are still not making enough noise.

FELIX. That's Ned's department in our family. I'm not feeling too political at the moment.

EMMA. I'd like to try a treatment of several chemotherapies used together. It's milder than others. I've had to try a lot of different things and a lot of people have died in the process, a bit faster than they might have died but not by much. There's a lot of pain and deterioration in this disease. I'm sorry but you have to know that. Everybody has to know that. You're an early case.

FELIX. I assume that's hopeful.

EMMA. It's always better early.

FELIX. It also takes longer until you die.

EMMA. Yes. You can look at it that way.

FELIX. Ned says you're guaranteed not to let anyone have any self-pity.

EMMA. I know he said that to me and I know he meant it kindly but I resent it, so don't repeat it. We all spend a lot of time wanting to be like everyone else.

FELIX. Do you want a second opinion?

EMMA. Feel free. But I'll say this about my fellow hospitals, which I shouldn't: you won't get particularly good care anywhere, maybe not even here. At . . .I'll call it Hospital A, you'll come under a group of mad scientists, research fanatics, who will try almost anything and if you die you die. You'll rarely see the same doctor twice; you'll just be a statistic for their computer – which they won't share with anyone else, by the way; there's not much sharing going on, never is – you'll be a true guinea pig. At Hospital B, they decided they really didn't want to get involved with this, it's too messy, and they're right, so you'll be overlooked by the least informed of doctors. C is like *The New York Times* and our friends everywhere: square, righteous, superior, and embarrassed by this disease and this entire epidemic. D is Catholic. E is Jewish. F is . . . Why am I telling you this? I must be insane. But the situation is insane.

FELIX. I guess we better get started.

EMMA. We have. You'll come to me once a week. There are going to be a lot of tests, a lot of blood tests, a lot of waiting. You might consider starting *War and Peace*. My secretary will give you a long list of dos and don'ts. Now, Felix, you understand your body no longer has any effective mechanism for fighting off anything?

FELIX. I'm going to be all right, you know.

EMMA. Good. That's the right attitude.

FELIX. No, I'm going to be the one who kicks it. I've always been lucky.

EMMA. Good.

FELIX. I guess everyone says that. Well, I'm going to be the one. I wanted a job on the *Times*, I got it. I wanted Ned . . . Have I given it to Ned?

EMMA. I don't know.

FELIX. Can he catch it from me now?

EMMA. We just don't know.

FELIX. Did he give it to me?

EMMA. Only one out of a hundred adults infected with the polio virus gets it; virtually everybody infected with rabies dies. One person has a cold, hepatitis – sometimes the partner catches it, sometimes not. I don't think we'll ever know why.

FELIX. No more making love?

EMMA. Right.

FELIX. Some gay doctors are saying it's okay if you use rubbers.

EMMA. I know they are.

FELIX. Can we kiss?

EMMA. I don't know.

FELIX (after a long pause). I want my mother.

EMMA. Where is she?

FELIX. She's dead. We never got along anyway.

EMMA. I'm going to do my damnedest, Felix. (She starts to leave.)

FELIX. Hey, Doc . . . I'll bet you say that to all the boys. Guess what? I've got a life-threatening disease.

Scene Eleven

A small, crowded office. Many phones are ringing. TOMMY is on two at once: MICKEY, going crazy, is on another, trying to understand and hear in the din: and GRADY, a volunteer, also on a phone, is trying to pass papers and information to either. Another volunteer, LENNIE, is also on the phone.

GRADY. GMHC.

LENNIE. GMHC.

MICKEY. Tommy, why hasn't Ned showed up?

TOMMY. Search me, Sugar. Hello, GMHC.

GRADY. No, we don't recommend that hospital.

MICKEY. Hello, GMHC.

BRUCE (entering, dressed as from the office, with his attaché case, picking up a ringing phone). Hello, GMHC.

LENNIE. It was mailed to you a month ago.

BRUCE. Hey, you guys, they've discovered the first case in Moscow.

TOMMY. Oh my God, faggots in Moscow. Who would believe it?

MICKEY. No, a cure has not been found; I don't care what you heard on the local news.

GRADY. GMHC.

MICKEY. Hello, GMHC.

GRADY. I only joined to find a boyfriend.

LENNIE. Hello, GMHC. Oh, hi, Mom.

MICKEY. Hello. Just a moment. It's another theory call. Okay, go ahead. Uranus . . . ? (*Writing it down.*)

GRADY. Whose asshole you talking about, Mickey?

MICKEY. Grady!

TOMMY (*to* GRADY). I thought your friend, little Vinnie, was going to show up today.

GRADY. He had to go to the gym. That's how he keeps his hot little body.

TOMMY. A hot body is always attached to an asshole.

MICKEY (*reading into the phone what he's written*). 'Mystical electromagnetic fields ruled by the planet Uranus?' Yes, well, we'll certainly keep that in mind. Thank you for calling and sharing that with us.

GRADY. Harry's in a pay phone at the Post Office.

MICKEY. Get a number, we'll call him back.

GRADY (*into the phone*). Give me the number, I'll call you back.

TOMMY (*into one phone*). Philip, can you hold on? (*Into the second phone.*) Graciella, you tell Senor Hiram I've been holding for *diez minutos* and he called me. *Si, si!* (*Into the first phone.*) *You* know where St Vincent's is? You get your ass there fast! I'll send you a crisis counsellor later today. I know you're scared, honey, but just get there.

GRADY *hands* MICKEY *Harry's phone number.* TOMMY *has hung up one phone.*

MICKEY. Well, call him back!

TOMMY. Mickey, do we have a crisis counsellor we can send to St V's around six o'clock?

MICKEY *(consulting a chart on a wall)*. No.

TOMMY. Shit. *(To* BRUCE.*)* Hi, Bossman.

BRUCE *(answering a ringing phone)*. Hello. How ya doin'! *(To the room.)* It's Kessler in San Francisco.

GRADY *(into his phone)*. Louder, Harry! It's a madhouse. None of the volunteers showed up.

MICKEY *(on his phone)*. Oh, dear.

BRUCE *(on his)*. No kidding.

GRADY. Oh, dear!

TOMMY *(picking up a ringing phone)*. Ned's not here yet.

BRUCE *(to the room)*. San Francisco's Mayor is giving four million dollars to their organisation. *(Into the phone.)* Well, we still haven't met our Mayor. We met with his assistant about four months ago.

TOMMY *(to* BRUCE*)*. Hiram called three days ago and left a message he found some money for us. Try and get him back.

MICKEY. We need to train some more crisis counsellors.

GRADY. What about me, Mick?

TOMMY *(standing up)*. Okay, get this! The *Times is* finally writing a big story. Twenty months after the epidemic has been declared, the *Times is* finally writing a big story. Word is that Craig Claiborne took someone high up out to lunch and told them they really had to write something, anything.

MICKEY. Who's writing it?

TOMMY. Some lady in Baltimore.

MICKEY. Makes sense. *(His phone rings.)* Hello.

GRADY *(still on his phone)*. Oh, dear.

TOMMY. Grady, darling, what the fuck are you oh-dearing about?

GRADY *(dropping his bombshell to* BRUCE*)*. Bruce – Harry says the Post Office won't accept our mailing.

BRUCE. What! *(Into the phone.)* Got to go.

He slams the phone down and grabs GRADY's.

Harry, what's the problem?

MICKEY *(into his phone)*. That's awful.

GRADY *(into his phone)*. They can't do that to us!

TOMMY *(who hadn't heard* GRADY*)*. What is it now?

GRADY. Harry went to the Post Office with the fifty-seven cartons of our new Newsletters –

TOMMY. Sugar, I sent him there!

GRADY. Well, they're not going anywhere.

BRUCE (*to* TOMMY). The Post Office won't accept them because we just used our initials.

TOMMY. So what?

BRUCE. In order to get tax-exemption we have to use our full name.

TOMMY. There is a certain amount of irony in all this, though not right now.

GRADY. He's double-parked and his volunteers had to go home.

TOMMY. Grady, dear, would you go help him out.

GRADY. No.

TOMMY AND MICKEY. Grady!

GRADY. No! Why do I always have to do the garbage stuff?

MICKEY. Grady!

GRADY. Give me the phone. (*Into the phone*.) Hold on, Harry, I'm coming to help you. (*To* TOMMY:) Give me cab fare.

TOMMY. Ride the rail, boy.

BRUCE (*into the phone*). Harry, someone's coming. (*Whispering to* TOMMY.) What's his name?

TOMMY AND MICKEY. Grady!

GRADY *goes*.

BRUCE (*into the phone*). Harry, bring them back. I want to fight this further somewhere. I'm sorry, I know it's a schlepp.

TOMMY. So this means we either pay full rate or embarrass their mailmen. Sorry, honey, I couldn't resist. (*Into the phone*.) Graciella! (*To the room.*) How do you say I've been holding twenty minutes in Spanish? (*Into the phone*.) City Hall is an equal-opportunity employer, doesn't that mean you all have to learn English? (*He hangs up.*)

MICKEY (*hanging up*). That was Atlanta. They're reporting thirty cases a week now nationally.

BRUCE. Thirty?

TOMMY. The CDC are filthy liars. What's wrong with those boys? We log forty cases a week in this office alone.

BRUCE. Forty?

TOMMY. Forty.

MICKEY. Thirty.

BRUCE *(trying to decide how to enter this on the wall chart). So* that's thirty nationally, forty in this office alone.

TOMMY. You heard what I said. *(Dialling, then into the phone.)* Hi. Pick up for us, will you, dears? We need a little rest. Thank *you. (Hangs up.)*

There is a long moment of silence, strange now without the ringing phones. TOMMY *lights a cigarette and sits back.* MICKEY *tries to concentrate on some paperwork.* BRUCE *is at the wall entering figures on charts.*

BRUCE. Mickey . . . aren't you supposed to be in Rio?

MICKEY. Where's Ned?

TOMMY. He should be here by now.

BRUCE. I don't want to see him.

MICKEY. I need to talk to him. I don't want to lose my job because Ned doesn't like sex very much. He's coming on like Jesus Christ, as if he never took a lover himself.

BRUCE. Rio. Why aren't you in Rio?

MICKEY. I was in Rio. I'm tired. I need a rest.

BRUCE. We're all exhausted.

TOMMY. You're the President; you can't have a rest.

MICKEY. I work all day for the city writing stuff on breastfeeding versus formula and how to stay calm if you have herpes and I work all night on our Newsletter and my health columns for the *Native* and I can't take it any more. Now this . . .

TOMMY. Take it slowly.

BRUCE. Now what?

MICKEY. I was in Rio, Gregory and I are in Rio, we just got there, day before yesterday, I get a phone call, from Hiram's office.

BRUCE. In Rio?

MICKEY. I'm told to be at a meeting in his office right away, this morning.

BRUCE. What kind of meeting? Why didn't you call me and I could have checked it out?

MICKEY. Because, unfortunately, you are not my boss.

BRUCE. What kind of meeting?

MICKEY. I don't know. I get to City Hall, he keeps me waiting forever; finally the Commissioner comes, my boss; and he said I hope you had a nice vacation, and went inside, into Hiram's office; and I waited some more, and the Commissioner comes out and says, Hiram doesn't want to see you any more. I said, please, sir, then why did he make me come all the way back from Rio? He said, your vacation isn't over? I said, no sir, I was just there one day. I wanted to scream I haven't slept in two days, you dumb fuck! but I didn't. What I said was, sir, does this mean I'm fired? And the Commissioner said, no, I don't think he means that, and he left.

NED *enters, unnoticed.*

Ned's article in the *Native* attacking Hiram came out last week. I love sex! I worship men! I don't think Ned does. I don't think Ned likes himself. I –

NED. What are you trying to say, Mickey?

MICKEY. You keep trying to make us say things that we don't want to say! And I don't think we can afford to make so many enemies before we have enough friends.

NED. We'll never have enough friends. We have to accept that. And why does what I say mean I don't like myself? Why is anything I'm saying compared to anything but common sense? When are we going to have this out once and for all? How many cases a week now?

MICKEY. Thirty . . . forty . . .

NED. Reinhard dead, Craig dead, Albert sick, Felix not getting any better . . . Richie Faro just died.

MICKEY. Richie!

NED. That guy Ray Schwartz just committed suicide. Terry's calling all his friends from under his oxygen tent to say goodbye. Soon we're going to be blamed for not doing anything to help ourselves. When are we going to admit we might be spreading this? We have simply fucked ourselves silly for years and years, and sometimes we've done it in the filthiest places.

TOMMY. Some of us have never been to places like that, Ned.

NED. Well, good for you, Tommy. Maybe you haven't, but others you've been with have, so what's the difference?

TOMMY *(holding up his cigarette).* It's my right to kill myself.

NED. But it is not your right to kill me. This is not a civil rights issue, this is a contagion issue.

BRUCE. We don't know that yet, and until they discover the virus, we're not certain where this is coming from.

NED. We know enough to cool it for a while! And save lives while we do. All it takes is one wrong fuck. That's not promiscuity – that's bad luck.

TOMMY. All right, so it's back to kissing and cuddling and waiting around for Mr Right – who could be Mr Wrong. Maybe if they'd let us get married to begin with none of this would have happened at all. I think I'll call Dr Ruth.

MICKEY. Will you please stop!

TOMMY. Mick, are you all right?

MICKEY. I don't think so.

TOMMY. What's wrong? Tell Tommy.

MICKEY. Why can't they find the virus?

TOMMY. It takes time.

MICKEY. I can't take any more theories. I've written a column about every single one of them. Repeated infection by a virus, new appearance by a dormant virus, single virus, new virus, old virus, multi-virus, partial virus, latent virus, mutant virus, retrovirus . . .

TOMMY. Take it easy, honey.

MICKEY. And we mustn't forget fucking, sucking, kissing, blood, voodoo, drugs, poppers, needles, Africa, Haiti, Cuba, Blacks, amoebas, pigs, mosquitoes, monkeys, Uranus! . . . What if it isn't any of them?

TOMMY. I don't know.

MICKEY. What if it's something out of the blue. The Great Plague of London was caused by polluted drinking water from a pump nobody noticed. Maybe it's a genetic predisposition, or the theory of the herd – only so many of us will get it and then the pool's used up. What if it's monogamy? Bruce, you and I could actually be worse off because of constant bombardment of the virus from a single source – our own lovers! Maybe guys who go to the baths regularly have built up the best immunity! I don't know what to tell anybody. And everybody asks me. I don't know – who's right? I don't know – who's wrong? I feel so inadequate! How can we tell people to stop when it might turn out to be caused by – I don't know!

BRUCE. That's exactly how I feel.

MICKEY. And Ned keeps calling the Mayor a prick and Hiram a prick and the Commissioner a prick and the President and *The New York Times,* and that's the entire political structure of the entire United States! When are you going to stop your eternal name-calling at every person you see?

BRUCE. That's exactly how I feel.

MICKEY. But maybe he's right! And that scares me, too. Neddie, you scare me.

TOMMY. If I were you, I'd get back on that plane to Gregory and Rio immediately.

MICKEY. And who's going to pay my fare? And now my job. I don't make much, but it's enough to let me help out here. Where are all the gay Rockefellers? Do you think the President really wants this to happen? Do you think the CIA really has unleashed germ warfare to kill off all the queers Jerry Falwell doesn't want? Why should they help us; we're actually co-operating with them by dying?

NED. Mickey, try and hold on.

MICKEY. To what? I used to love my country. The *Native* received an anonymous letter describing top-secret Defense Department experiments at Fort Detrick, Maryland, that have produced a virus that can destroy the immune system. It's code name is Firm Hand. They started testing in 1978 – on a group of gays. I never used to believe shit like this before. They are going to persecute us! Cancel our health insurance. Test our blood to see if we're pure. Lock us up. Stone us in the streets. *(To* NED:) And you think I am killing people?

NED. Mickey, that is not what I –

MICKEY. Yes, you do! I know you do! I've spent fifteen years of my life fighting for our right to be free and make love whenever, wherever . . . And you're telling me that all those years of what being gay stood for is wrong . . . and I'm a murderer. We have been so oppressed! Don't you remember how it was? Can't you see how important it is for us to love openly, without hiding and without guilt? We were a bunch of funny-looking fellows who grew up in sheer misery and one day we fell into the orgy rooms and we thought we'd found heaven. And we would teach the world how wonderful heaven can be. We would lead the way. We would be good for something new. Can't you see that? Can't you?

TOMMY. I see that. I do, Mickey. Come on – I'm taking you home now.

MICKEY. When I left Hiram's office I went to the top of the Empire State Building to jump off.

TOMMY *(going to get* MICKEY's *coat)*. Mickey. I'm taking you home right now! Let's go.

MICKEY. You can jump off from there if no one is looking. Ned, I'm not a murderer. All my life I've been hated. For one reason or another. For being short. For being Jewish. Jerry Falwell mails out millions of pictures of two men kissing as if that was the most awful sight you could see. Tell everybody we were wrong. And I'm sorry. Someday someone will come along and put the knife in you and say everything you fought for all this time is . . . shit! *(He has made a furious, running lunge for* NED, *but* TOMMY *catches him and cradles him in his arms.)*

BRUCE. Need any help?

TOMMY. Get my coat. *(To* MICKEY.*)* You're just a little tired that's all, a little bit yelled out. We've got a lot of different styles that don't quite mesh. We've got ourselves a lot of bereavement overload. Tommy's taking you home.

MICKEY. No. Don't take me home. I'm afraid I might do something. Take me to St Vincent's. I'm just afraid.

TOMMY. I'll take you wherever you want to go. *(To* BRUCE *and* NED.*)* Okay, you two, no more apologising and no more fucking excuses. You two better start accommodating and talking to each other now. Or we're in big trouble.

MICKEY. We're the fighters, aren't we?

TOMMY. You bet, sweetness. And you're a hero. Whether you know it or not. You're our first hero.

TOMMY *and* MICKEY *leave. There is a long moment of silence.*

NED. We're all going to go crazy, living this epidemic every minute, while the rest of the world goes on out there, all around us, as if nothing is happening, going on with their own lives and not knowing what it's like, what we're going through. We're living through war, but where they're living it's peacetime, and we're all in the same country.

BRUCE. Do you want to be President?

NED. I just want Felix to live. *(Nodding in understanding.)* What are we going to do, you and me?

BRUCE. I don't know.

NED. I don't think straight men have the same set of problems when they're running General Motors.

A phone on TOMMY's *desk rings.*

Hello Hiram, old buddy, how they hanging? I want to talk to

you, too. *(He listens, then hangs up softly.)* Tommy's right. All yelled out. You ready?

BRUCE. Yes.

NED. The Mayor has found a secret little fund for giving away money. But we're not allowed to tell anyone where we got it. If word gets out we've told, we won't get it.

BRUCE. How much?

NED. Nine thousand dollars.

BRUCE. Ned, Albert is dead.

NED. Oh, no.

BRUCE. He died . . . What's today?

NED. Wednesday.

BRUCE. He's been dead a week.

NED. I didn't know he was so close.

BRUCE. No one did. He wouldn't tell anyone. Do you know why? Because of me. Because he knows I'm so scared I'm some sort of carrier. This makes three people I've been with who are dead. I went to Emma and I begged her please test me somehow, please tell me if I'm giving this to people. And she said she couldn't, there isn't any way they can find out anything because they still don't know what they're looking for. Albert, I think I loved him best of all, and he went so fast. His mother wanted him back in Phoenix before he died, this was last week when it was obvious, so I get permission from Emma and bundle him all up and take him to the plane in an ambulance. The pilot wouldn't take off and I refused to leave the plane – you would have been proud of me – so finally they get another pilot. Then, after we take off, Albert loses his mind, not recognising me, not knowing where he is or that he's going home, and then, right there, on the plane, he becomes . . . incontinent. He starts doing it in his pants and all over the seat; shit, piss, everything. I pulled down my suitcase and yanked out whatever clothes were in there and I start mopping him up as best I can, and all these people are staring at us and moving away in droves and . . . I ram all these clothes back in the suitcase and I sat there holding his hand, saying, 'Albert, please, no more, hold it in, man, I beg you, just for us, for Bruce and Albert.' And when we got to Phoenix, there's a police van waiting for us and all the police are in complete protective rubber clothing, they looked like fucking astronauts, and by the time we got to the hospital where his mother had fixed up his room real nice, Albert was dead.

NED *starts towards him.*

Wait. It gets worse. The hospital doctors refused to examine him to put a cause of death on the death certificate, and without a death certificate, the undertakers wouldn't take him away, and neither would the police. Finally, some orderly comes in and stuffs Albert in a heavy-duty Glad Bag and motions us with his finger to follow and he puts him out in the back alley with the garbage. He says, 'Hey, man. See what a big favour I've done for you, I got him out. I want fifty bucks.' I paid him, and then his mother and I carried the bag to her car and we finally found a black undertaker who cremated him for a thousand dollars, no questions asked.

NED *crosses to* BRUCE *and embraces him;* BRUCE *puts his arms around* NED.

Would you and Felix mind if I spent the night on your sofa? Just one night. I don't want to go home.

Scene Twelve

EMMA *sits alone in a spotlight, facing a* DOCTOR *who stands at a distance, perhaps in the audience. She holds a number of files on her lap, or they are placed in a carrier attached to her wheelchair.*

EXAMINING DOCTOR. Dr Brookner, the Government's position is this. There are several million dollars in the pipeline, five to be exact, for which we have received some fifty-five million dollars' worth of requests – all the way from a doctor in North Dakota who desires to study the semen of pigs to the health reporter on Long Island who is convinced this is being transmitted by dogs and the reason so many gay men are contracting it is because they have so many dogs.

EMMA. Five million dollars doesn't seem quite right for some two thousand cases. The Government spent twenty million investigating seven deaths from Tylenol. We are now almost into the third year of this epidemic.

EXAMINING DOCTOR. Unfortunately the President has threatened to veto. As you know, he's gone on record as being unalterably and irrevocably opposed to anything that might be construed as an endorsement of homosexuality. Naturally, this has slowed things down.

EMMA. Naturally. It looks like we've got a pretty successful stalemate going on here.

EXAMINING DOCTOR. Well, that's not what we're here to discuss today, is it?

EMMA. I don't think I'm going to enjoy hearing what I think I'm about to hear. But go ahead. At your own peril.

EXAMINING DOCTOR. We have decided to reject your application for funding.

EMMA. Oh? I would like to hear your reasons.

EXAMINING DOCTOR. We felt the direction of your thinking was imprecise and unfocused.

EMMA. Could you be a little more precise?

EXAMINING DOCTOR. I beg your pardon?

EMMA. You don't know what's going on any more than I do. My guess is as good as anybody's. Why are you blocking my efforts?

EXAMINING DOCTOR. Dr Brookner, since you first became involved with this – and we pay tribute to you as a pioneer, one of the few courageous pioneers – there have been other investigators . . . Quite frankly, it's no longer just your disease, though you seem to think it is.

EMMA. Oh, I do, do I? And you're here to take it away from me, is that it? Well, I'll let you in on a little secret, Doctor. You can have it. I didn't want it in the first place. You think it's my good fortune to have the privilege of watching young men die? Oh, what's the use! What am I arguing with you for? You don't know enough medicine to treat a mouse. You don't know enough science to study boiled water. How dare you come and judge me?

EXAMINING DOCTOR. We only serve on this panel at the behest of Dr Joost.

EMMA. Another idiot. And, by the way, a closeted homosexual who is doing everything in his power to sweep this under the rug, and I vowed I'd never say that in public. How does it always happen that all the idiots are always on your team? You guys have all the money, call the shots, shut everybody out, and then operate behind closed doors. I am taking care of more victims of this epidemic than anyone in the world. We have more accumulated test results, more data, more frozen blood samples, more experience! How can you not fund my research or invite me to participate in yours? A promising virus has already been discovered – in France. Why are we being told not to co-operate with the French? Why are you refusing to co-operate with the French? Just so you can steal a Nobel Prize? Your National Institutes of Health received my first request for research money two years ago. It took you one year just to print up application forms. It's taken you two and a half years from my first reported case just to show up here to take a look. The paltry amount of money you are making us beg for – from the four billion dollars you are given each and every year – won't come to anyone until only God knows when. Any way you add all this up, it is an unconscionable delay and has never, never existed in any other health emergency during this entire century. While something is being passed around that causes death. We are enduring an epidemic of death. Women have been discovered to have it in Africa – where it is clearly transmitted heterosexually. It is only a question of time. We could all be dead before you do anything. You want my patients? Take them! TAKE THEM! *(She starts hurling her folders and papers at him, out into space.)* Just do something for them! You're fucking right I'm imprecise and unfocused. And you are all idiots!

Scene Thirteen

A big empty room, which will be the organisation's new offices. BRUCE is walking around by himself. NED comes in from upstairs.

NED. This is perfect for our new offices. The room upstairs is just as big. And it's cheap.

BRUCE. How come, do you think?

NED. Didn't Tommy tell you? After he found it, he ran into the owner in a gay bar who confessed, after a few beers, his best friend is sick. Did you see us on TV picketing the Mayor yesterday in all that rain?

BRUCE. Yes.

NED. How'd we look?

BRUCE. All wet.

NED. He's got four more hours to go. Our letter threatened if he didn't meet with us by the end of the day we'd escalate the civil disobedience. Mel found this huge straight black guy who trained with Martin Luther King. He's teaching us how to tie up the bridge and tunnel traffic. Don't worry – a bunch of us are doing this on our own.

BRUCE. Tommy got the call.

NED. Tommy? Why didn't you tell me? When did they call?

BRUCE. This morning.

NED. When's the meeting?

BRUCE. Tomorrow.

NED. You see. It works! What time?

BRUCE. Eight a.m.

NED. For the Mayor I'll get up early.

BRUCE. We can only bring ten people. Hiram's orders.

NED. Who's going?

BRUCE. The Community Council sends two, the Network sends two, the Task Force sends two, we send two, and two patients.

NED. I'll pick you up at seven-thirty and we can share a cab.

BRUCE. You remember we elected Tommy Executive Director.

NED. I'm going.

BRUCE. We can only bring two.

NED. You just call Hiram and tell him we're bringing three.

BRUCE. The list of names has already been phoned in. It's too late.

NED. So I'll just go. What are they going to do? Kick me out? Already phoned in? Too late? Why is everything so final? Why is all this being done behind my back? How dare you make this decision without consulting me?

BRUCE. Ned . . .

NED. I wrote that letter, I got sixty gay organisations to sign it, I organised the picketing when the Mayor wouldn't respond, that meeting is mine! It's happening because of me! It took me twenty-one months to arrange it and, God damn it, I'm going to go!

BRUCE. You're not the whole organisation.

NED. What does that mean? Why didn't Tommy tell me?

BRUCE. I told him not to.

NED. You what?

BRUCE. I wanted to poll the Board.

NED. Behind my back – what kind of betrayal is going on behind my back? I'm on the Board, you didn't poll me. I am going to that meeting representing this organisation that I have spent every minute of my life fighting for and that was started in my living-room, or I quit!

BRUCE. I told them I didn't think you'd accept their decision.

NED (*as it sinks in*). You would let me quit? You didn't have to poll the Board. If you wanted to take me, you'd take me. I embarrass you.

BRUCE. Yes, you do. The Mayor's finally meeting with us and we all feel we now have a chance to –

NED. A chance to kiss his ass?

BRUCE. We want to work from the inside now that we have the contact.

NED. It won't work. Did you get this meeting by kissing his ass? He's the one person most responsible for letting this epidemic get so out of control. If he'd responded with one ounce of compassion when we first tried to reach him, we'd have saved two years. You'll see . . . We have over half a million dollars. The *Times* is finally writing about us. Why are you willing to let me go when I've been so effective? When you need me most?

BRUCE. You . . . you're a bully. If the Board doesn't agree with you, you always threaten to leave. You never listen to us. I can't work with you any more.

NED. And you're strangling this organisation with your fear and your conservatism. The organisation I promised everyone would fight for them isn't fighting at all.

BRUCE. We just feel you can't tell people how to live.

NED. Drop that! Just drop it! The cases are still doubling every six months. Of course we have to tell people how to live. Or else there won't be any people left! Did you ever consider it could get so bad they'll quarantine us or put us in camps?

BRUCE. Oh, they will not.

NED. It's happened before. It's all happened before. History is worth shit. I swear to God I now understand . . . Is this how so many people just walked into gas chambers? But at least they identified themselves to each other and to the world.

BRUCE. You can't call people gay who don't want to be.

NED. Bruce – after you're dead, it doesn't make any difference.

BRUCE (*takes a letter out of his pocket*). The Board wanted me to read you this letter. 'We are circulating this letter widely among people of judgment and good sense in our community. We take this action to try to combat your damage, wrought, so far as we can see, by your having no scruples whatever. You are on a colossal ego trip we must curtail. To manipulate fear, as you have done repeatedly in your "merchandising" of this epidemic, is to us the gesture of barbarism. To exploit the deaths of gay men, as you have done in publications all over America, is to us an act of inexcusable vandalism. And to attempt to justify your bursts of outrageous temper as "part of what it means to be Jewish" is past our comprehending. And, after years of liberation, you have helped make sex dirty again for us – terrible and forbidden. We are more angry at you than ever in our lives toward anyone. We think you want to lead us all. Well, we do not want you to. In accordance with our by-laws as drawn up by Weeks, Frankel, Levinstein, Mr Ned Weeks is hereby removed as a director. We beg that you leave us quietly and not destroy us and what good work we manage despite your disapproval. In closing, please know we always welcome your input, advice, and help.'

BRUCE *tries to hand* NED *the letter*. NED *won't take it*. BRUCE *tries to put it in* NED's *breast pocket*. NED *deflects* BRUCE's *hand*.

NED. I belong to a culture that includes Proust, Henry James, Tchaikovsky, Cole Porter, Plato, Socrates, Aristotle, Alexander the Great, Michelangelo, Leonardo da Vinci, Christopher Marlowe, Walt Whitman, Herman Melville, Tennessee Williams, Byron, E.M. Forster, Lorca, Auden, Francis Bacon, James Baldwin, Harry Stack Sullivan, John Maynard Keynes, Dag Hammarskjöld . . . These were not invisible men. Poor Bruce. Poor frightened Bruce. Once upon a time you wanted to be a soldier. Bruce, did you know that it was an openly gay Englishman who was as responsible as any man for winning the Second World War? His name was Alan Turing and he cracked the German's Enigma code so the Allies knew in advance what the Nazis were going to do – and when the war was over he committed suicide he was so hounded for being gay. Why don't they teach any of this in the schools? If they did, maybe he wouldn't have killed himself and maybe you wouldn't be so terrified of who you are. The only way we'll have real pride is when we demand recognition of a culture that isn't just sexual. It's all there – all through history we've been there; but we have to claim it, and identify who was in it, and articulate what's in our minds and hearts and all our creative contributions to this earth. And until we do that, and until we organise ourselves block by neighbourhood by city by state into a united visible community that fights back, we're doomed. That's how I want to be defined as one of the men who fought the war. Being defined by our cocks is literally killing us. Must we all be reduced to becoming our own murderers? Why couldn't you and I, Bruce Niles and Ned Weeks, have been leaders in creating a new definition of what it means to be gay? I blame myself as much as you. Bruce, I know I'm an asshole. But, please, I beg you, don't shut me out.

BRUCE *starts to leave then stops and comes to* NED. *He puts his hand on his cheek, perhaps kisses him, and then leaves him standing alone.*

Scene Fourteen

NED's *apartment.* FELIX is *sitting on the floor. He has been eating junk food.* NED *comes in carrying a bag of groceries.*

NED. Why are you sitting on the floor?

FELIX. I fell down trying to get from there to here.

NED. Let's put you to bed.

FELIX. Don't touch me! I'm so ugly. I cannot stand it when you look at my body.

NED. Do you have any nausea from the chemo?

FELIX. Yes. I threw it all up. You don't have to let me stay here with you. This is horrible for you.

NED (*touching* FELIX's *hair*). No fallout yet. Phil looks cute shaved. I'm hungry. How about you? Can you eat a little? Please. You've got to eat. Soup . . . something light . . . I've bought dinner.

FELIX. Emma says a cure won't come until the next century. Emma says it's years till a vaccine, which won't do me any good anyway. Emma says the incubation period might be up to three, ten, twenty years.

NED. Emma says you've got to eat.

FELIX. I looked at all my datebooks and no one else I slept with is sick. That I know of. Maybe it was you. Maybe you've been a carrier for twenty years. Or maybe now you only have three years to go.

NED. Felix, we don't need to do this again to each other.

FELIX. Whoever thought you'd die from making love?

NED. Did Emma also tell you that research at the NIH has finally started? That something is now possible. We have to hope.

FELIX. Oh, do we?

NED. Yes, we do.

FELIX. And how am I supposed to do that? You Jewish boys who think you can always make everything right – that the world can always be a better place. Did I tell you the *Times* is running an editorial this Sunday entitled 'The Slow Response'? And you're right: I didn't have anything to do with it.

NED. Why are you doing this? Why are you eating this shit? Twinkies, potato chips . . . You know how important it is to watch your nutrition. You're supposed to eat right.

FELIX. I have a life expectancy of ten more minutes I'm going to eat what I want to eat. Ned, it's going to get messier any day now and I don't want to make you see it.

NED. Nobody makes me do anything; you should know that better than anybody else by now. What are you going to do? Sit on the floor for the rest of your life? We have a bed in the other room. You could listen to those relaxation tapes we bought you three months ago. You haven't used them at all. Do you hear me?

FELIX. Yes, I hear you. That guy David who sold you the pig on Bleecker Street finally died. He took forever. They say he looked like someone out of Auschwitz. Do you hear me?

NED. No. Are you ready to get up yet? And eat something?

FELIX. No! – I've had over forty treatments. No! – I've had three, no four different types of chemo. No! – I've had interferon, a couple of kinds. I've had two different experimentals. Emma has spent more time on me than anyone else. None of it has done a thing. I've had to go into the hospital four times – and please God don't make me go back into hospital until I die. My illness has cost my – no! *The New York Times'* insurance company over $300,000. Eighty-five per cent of us are dead after two years, Alexander; it gets higher after three. Emma has lost so many patients they call her Dr Death. You cannot force the goddamn sun to come out.

NED. Felix, I am so sick of statistics, and numbers, and body counts, and howmanys, and Emma; and everyday, Felix, there are only more numbers, and fights – I am so sick of fighting, and bragging about fighting, and everybody's stupidity, and blindness, and intransigence, and guilt trips. You can't eat the food? Don't eat the food. Take your poison. I don't care. You can't get up off the floor – fine, stay there. I don't care. Fish – fish is good for you; we don't want any of that, do we?

Item by item, he throws the food on the floor.

No green salad. No broccoli; we don't want any of that, no, sir.

No bread with seven grains. Who would ever want any milk?
You might get some calcium in your bones.

The carton of milk explodes when it hits the floor.

You want to die, Felix? Die!

NED *retreats to a far corner. After a moment,* FELIX *crawls
through the milk, takes an item of food, which he pulls along
with his hand, and with extreme effort makes his way across to*
NED.

Felix, please don't leave me.

Scene Fifteen

BEN's *office.* FELIX, *with great effort, walks towards him.
Though he looks terrible,* FELIX *has a bit of his old twinkle.*

FELIX. Thank you for seeing me. Your brother and I are lovers.
I'm dying and I need to make a will. Oh, I know Neddie hasn't
been talking to you; our excuse is we've sort of been
preoccupied. It's a little hard on us, isn't it, his kind of love,
because we disappoint him so. But it is love. I hope you know
that. I haven't very much time left. I want to leave everything to
Ned. I've written it all down.

BEN (*taking the piece of paper from* FELIX *and studying it*). Do
you have any family, Felix?

FELIX. My parents are dead. I had a wife.

BEN. You had a wife?

FELIX. Yes. Here's the divorce. (*He hands* BEN *another piece of
paper.*) And I have a son. Here's . . . She has custody.

(*He hands over yet another piece of paper.*)

BEN. Does she know you're ill?

FELIX. Yes. I called and we've said our goodbyes. She doesn't
want anything from me. She was actually rather pleasant.
Although she wouldn't let me talk to my boy.

BEN. How is my brother?

FELIX. Well, he blames himself, of course, for everything from
my dying to the state of the entire world. But he's not talking so
much these days, believe it or not. You must be as stubborn as
he is – not to have called.

BEN. I think of doing it every day. I'm sorry I didn't know you were ill. I'll call him right away.

FELIX. He's up at Yale for the week. He's in terrible shape. He was thrown out of the organisation he loved so much. After almost three years he sits at home all day, flagellating himself awfully because he thinks he's failed some essential test – plus my getting near the end and you two still not talking to each other.

BEN. Ned was thrown out of his own organisation?

FELIX. Yes.

BEN. Felix, I wish we could have met sooner.

FELIX. I haven't much, except a beautiful piece of land on the Cape in Wellfleet on a hill overlooking the Atlantic Ocean. Ned doesn't know about it. It was to have been a surprise, we'd live there together in the house he always wanted. I also have an insurance policy with the *Times*. I'm a reporter for *The New York Times*.

BEN. You work for the *Times*?

FELIX. Yes. Fashion. La-de-da. It's meant to come to my next of kin. I've specified Ned. I'm afraid they might not give it to him.

BEN. If he is listed as the beneficiary, they must.

FELIX. But what if they don't?

BEN. I assure you I will fight to see that he gets it.

FELIX. I was hoping you'd say that. Can I sign my will now, please, in case I don't have time to see you again?

BEN. This will be quite legal. We can stop by one of my associates' offices and get it properly witnessed as you sign it.

FELIX. My little piece of paper is legal? Then why did you go to law school?

BEN. I sometimes wonder. You know, Felix, I think of leaving here, too, because I don't think anybody is listening to me either. And I set all this up as well.

A hospital bed is wheeled into stage centre by two ORDERLIES, *wearing masks and gloves.*

I understand that the virus had finally been discovered in Washington .

FELIX. The story is they couldn't find it, so after fifteen months they stole it from the French and renamed it. With who knows how many million of us now exposed . . . Oh, there is not a good word to be said for anybody's behaviour in this whole mess. Then could you help me get a taxi, please? I have to get to the airport.

BEN. The airport?

FELIX. I'm going to Rumania to see their famous woman doctor. A desperation tactic, Tommy would call it. Does flying Bucharest Airlines inspire you with any confidence?

Scene Sixteen

FELIX's *hospital room.* FELIX *lies in bed.* NED *enters.*

FELIX. I should be wearing something white.

NED. You are.

FELIX. It should be something Perry Ellis ran up for me personally.

NED (*as* FELIX *presses a piece of rock into his hand*). What's this?

FELIX. From my trip. I forgot to give it to you. This is a piece of rock from Dracula's castle.

NED. Reminded you of me, did it?

FELIX. To remind you of me. Please learn to fight again.

NED. I went to a meeting at the Bishop's. All the gay leaders were there, including Bruce and Tommy. I wasn't allowed in. I went into the men's room of the rectory and the Bishop came in and as we stood there peeing side by side I screamed at him, 'What kind of house of God are we in?'

FELIX. Don't lose that anger. Just have a little more patience and forgiveness. For yourself as well.

NED. What am I ever going to do without you?

FELIX. Finish writing something. Okay?

NED. Okay.

FELIX. Promise?

NED. I promise.

FELIX. Okay. It better be good.

BEN *enters the scene.*

Hello, Ben.

BEN. Hello, Felix.

Before NED *can do more than register his surprise at seeing* BEN, EMMA *enters and comes to the side of the bed.*

FELIX. Emma, could we start. Please hurry.

EMMA. Dearly beloved we are gathered here together in the sight of God to join together these two men. They love each other very much and want to be married somehow in the presence of their family before Felix dies. I can see no objection. This is my hospital, my church. Do you, Felix —

FELIX. Hurry . . .

EMMA. Do you, Felix Turner, take you Ned Weeks . . .

FELIX. Alexander.

EMMA . . . . to be your . . .

FELIX. Lover. My lover. I do.

NED. I do.

FELIX is *dead.* EMMA, *who has been holding* FELIX's *hand and monitoring his pulse, places his hand on his body. She leaves. The two* ORDERLIES *enter and push the hospital bed through all the accumulated mess, off stage.*

He always wanted me to take him to your new house in the country. Just the four of us.

BEN. Ned, I'm sorry. For Felix . . . and for other things.

NED. Why didn't I fight harder! Why didn't I picket the White House, all by myself if nobody would come? Or go on a hunger strike? I forgot to tell him something. Felix, when they invited me to Gay Week at Yale, they had a dance . . . In my old college dining-hall, just across the campus from that tiny freshman room where I wanted to kill myself because I thought I was the only gay man in the world – they had a dance. Felix, there were six hundred young men and women there. Smart, exceptional young men and women. And they asked me to speak and I quoted from your favourite poem,

> What mad Nijinsky wrote
> About Diaghilev
> Is true of the normal heart;
> For the error bred in the bone
> Of each woman and each man
> Craves what it cannot have,
> Not universal love
> But to be loved alone.

Thank you, Felix.

After a moment, BEN crosses to NED, and somehow they manage to kiss and embrace and hold on to each other.

The End